Wakefield Press

CRIME

it can happen to you

Jo Robinson

CRIME

it can happen to you

THE STORY OF VICTIM SUPPORT SERVICE

JO ROBINSON

Wakefield
Press

Victim Support Service
in association with
Wakefield Press
1 The Parade West
Kent Town
South Australia 5067
www.wakefieldpress.com.au

First published 2004
Copyright © Jo Robinson, 2004

Designed and typeset by Ryan Paine, Wakefield Press
Printed and bound by Hyde Park Press

National Library of Australia
Cataloguing-in-publication entry

Robinson, Jo.
Crime, it can happen to you: the story of Victim Support Service.

Bibliography.
Includes index.
ISBN 1 86254 647 9.

1. Victim Support Service (S. Aust.). 2. Victims of crimes –
Services for – South Australia. 3. Crime prevention – South
Australia. I. Victim Support Service (S. Aust.). II. Title.

362.88099423

Wakefield Press thanks Fox Creek Wines
for their support.

To the memory of Raymond Wells Whitrod,

16 April 1915–12 June 2003

Fighting for the Right to Love

Children are trusting little souls
They have a natural desire to be loved
If they are neglected
Or their trust is abused
They build an invisible wall around
their heart
One they don't even know is there
But as they grow
So does the wall
So instead of love coming naturally
They have to fight for the right to love.

First part of a longer poem by 'Rain'

CONTENTS

Preface

When the victims of yet another murderous tragedy began to unravel, a healing force was born which bound people together. A single unnecessary death results in many victims who are left to face an uncertain future. The Truro murders sparked an eternal flame of remembrance, a burning desire for justice and the formation of the Victims Support Group.

Kathleen Bambridge, VSS volunteer

Be not overcome with evil, but overcome evil with good

Romans 7:21

At the beginning of this story there is evil. Evil is a dramatic word, which may have different connotations for each of us, but to many it is an enormous concept which almost defies comprehension. It suggests malicious forces and events beyond description and outside our control. Words like bad, wicked, criminal do not feel or sound sufficient. Evil emphasises our weakness and vulnerability in the face of overwhelming misfortune where the fallout can be endless. Evil, like good, can be life-changing.

We have all heard of, or experienced acts beyond our understanding, and at a subconscious level, recognise that around the world such events are occurring all the time. Normally, unless it's absolutely necessary, we don't know what they are and don't want to know. However, in these times of instant and continuous communication, the daily news can be more scary than any thriller novel or film. And that's the point – evil can be occurring even in our own neighbourhood without our knowledge.

When we come into direct contact with crime, we are shocked and paralysed with horror. We have difficulty understanding the incident and its outcomes. South Australians began to experience these emotions, first with the disappearance of the Beaumont children in 1966, the Gordon–Ratcliff abductions in 1973, and the Truro and 'family' murders in 1977–79. More recently, the community has experienced further anxiety, this time with the 'Missing Persons' trials, the first of which commenced in 2001.

In South Australia, as in the wider community, we struggle to come to terms with incomprehensible events. The victims may belong to other families but the shock waves affect our lives – these victims could belong to our family. People often say, when confronted with tragedy: 'You only expect to read about things like this in the newspapers, not that it will happen to you'.

Of course terrible things have happened to many other families in South Australia and elsewhere during this 25-year period, and the loss of each person through whatever reason, exerts a flow-through effect on many other lives. We grieve for all of them. Comprehension begins to falter when the loss is multiple, and especially when the victims are children or young people who should be looking forward to the life ahead of them.

In situations like these, cumulative evil sometimes has an opposite effect. Paralysis and outrage give way to action. People rally to challenge the threat, find solutions and take action. Inaction can be agony once the initial shock has worn off and there is often a tremendous surge of collective energy, which can be mobilised for good. This is what happened in South Australia in 1979.

This account does not pontificate on evil. On the contrary, it takes a look at how survivors of terrible events in South Australia have turned their anger and despair into action to help others in similar situations. It shows how the dictum 'Love thy neighbour', far from being simply a spiritual admonition, can provide practical help, comfort, emotional shelter, courage, humour and a future for those who need it.

It also illustrates how, a generation later, an organisation established by committed, caring people with energy and foresight, all volunteers, continues to motivate others to confront the effects of crime and join the organisation. Today, in many areas of the world, there is an even greater, ongoing need for compassion and practical assistance. With our 25 years experience behind us South Australia can lead the way.

It is self-evident that this book is not an academic thesis but a story about people. It has not been possible, nor have we attempted, to include every historical detail. It is an *overview* of 25 years of Victim Support Service history and achievements. It is written for everyone who has experienced crime, is concerned about victims or is interested in the available support services.

We hope that you will find it accessible and interesting and that you may be encouraged to take a closer look at VSS, either in Adelaide, through the regional branches or the interstate sister organisations, and perhaps become a member.

For the first 17 years the service was called VOCS, Victims of Crime Service. In 1996 it was renamed Victim Support Service Incorporated. To avoid confusion VSS is used throughout the book, except within direct quotes where VOCS is referred to specifically.

The arrangement of chapters is by subject matter rather than chronology, although there is some sequential continuity.

Where possible, we have gone directly to the sources of the information we have used. Years of newsletters, reports and oral histories have been studied and items extracted. We have incorporated passages from documents, poems and individual stories to convey as accurate a picture as possible of the philosophies and changing events in the organisation since 1979.

To achieve this, many direct quotes have been reproduced from the newsletters, especially where Ray Whitrod has expressed his feelings openly and often strongly. Ray played a pivotal role for many years and we have taken the liberty of using his first name, as was usual among the people with whom he worked. We have endeavoured not to interpret his words but let them speak for him.

Every effort has been made to contact contributors, but in some cases, poems were printed anonymously or with pseudonyms in early newsletters and we have been unable to trace the writers. We hope that the unacknowledged authors will accept the intended compliment. The role of Court Companions is illustrated through victim case histories which are all based on fact, but names and identifiable details have been changed to protect individuals.

We hope this glimpse of the development of VSS will widen your understanding and appreciation of the effect which crime has on people and communities, and what can be done to alleviate the distress. Since humour is considered to be therapeutic, we have included some of that too, in particular Ray's humour.

The VSS organisation continues to make an invaluable contribution to South Australians and maintains links with similar organisations interstate and overseas. This is a book you can dip in and out of and read aloud – the story of Australia's first Victim Support Service.

1. In the beginning …

Complacent ignorance is the greatest immorality.

Aldous Huxley

For me, complacent knowledge is a greater immorality.

Ray Whitrod

Welcome to Adelaide! Is the capital of South Australia just a city of pubs and churches? Well, no, that description is rarely applied to Adelaide these days, although it has been said that, in its colonial heyday, there were 118 pubs and 33 churches in the city square mile. Agreed, Adelaide is less frenetic than its counterparts in the eastern states and may appear self-indulgent, basking in its Mediterranean climate, but it has much of which to be proud.

The idea of South Australia as a free colony was born in Newgate Prison in London in 1827 where Edward Gibbon Wakefield, an educated young Quaker, was incarcerated for the abduction of a wealthy schoolgirl heiress. After his release, Wakefield, to achieve his aim, embarked upon a series of political manoeuvrings which took place over several years. Eventually in 1836, several ships containing new migrants and a variety of government officials, including Captain John Hindmarsh, the first Governor of the Colony, arrived on Kangaroo Island in South Australia.

The British Government appointed Colonel William Light who had been a career naval and army officer, as Surveyor-General and gave him total authority for determining the ideal location for the settlement. Since Light was not impressed by Kangaroo Island as a suitable site for the capital, he explored other parts of the coast before settling on Holdfast Bay for further, more detailed assessment.

Colonel Light had to withstand pressure from the new settlers who, unlike the populations in the other states, were not convicts but free migrants with strong opinions of their own. Much argument about choice of location for the establishment of the new city ensued, with a range of locations suggested – locations which today are Port Lincoln, Encounter Bay and Kangaroo Island. In spite of ill-health, Light resisted all suggestions to the contrary and selected the site for Adelaide alongside the rambling banks of the River Torrens in January 1837. He completed his survey of the proposed town in March of that year, a prodigious effort.

Shortly before his death he wrote: 'The reasons that led me to fix Adelaide where it is I do not expect to be generally understood or calmly judged of at present'.

The government buildings and a number of the residences including Light's own, were a flimsy mixture of timber and thatch, which burnt down two years later. Fortunately, the plans and survey records were stored in an iron safe and escaped destruction.

Colonel Light laid out the wide and spacious streets in a north-south and east-west grid, which today is still easy to access. The modern inner-city parklands are a mixture of lawns and roses, a Japanese garden and areas of native trees. Where once only farm animals grazed, they are a diminishing delight, having been eroded by city development.

In the past, a source of both pride and scornful comment has been South Australia's original non-convict settlement, but in today's multicultural and egalitarian society this is of little importance. Today we enjoy the range of cuisines and customs bestowed upon us by people from all walks of life and from many countries, most of whom have been encouraged or tolerated, at least until recently. Now with the increasing paranoia of terrorism we too seem to be joining the rest of the world in viewing some newcomers, and those of us who are different, with suspicion.

Adelaide considers itself cultured, although, as a venue, it is often over-looked by visiting performing companies from overseas and interstate due to the lack of appropriate performance space. Always self-confident, the city is proud of its festivals. There are festivals of arts, writers, roses, films, wine, ideas, food and many more, in Adelaide and the surrounding regions. A large proportion of the population is deeply committed to football and other sports. The majority of residents seem to consider Adelaide a good place in which to live and bring up children. For those with jobs, its many assets can add up to a comfortable lifestyle, but let us not forget the pockets of poverty and disadvantaged suburbs north and south of the capital.

Like many cities which are also bright and light and open, there is a dark and bleak underbelly. Despite elegant, leafy suburbs, beautiful hills and long stretches of ocean beaches, Adelaide has gradually become notorious worldwide for some of the most horrific cruelties inflicted against one human being by another.

Adelaide is also a city of abducted, lost children and serial murder. While such atrocities are shocking in any place, we in South Australia still find difficulty believing that events such as these can happen in our own backyards, on occasions, literally. The relative trust and innocence of earlier times were finally destroyed on Australia Day in 1966 when all three children from the Beaumont family disappeared from a popular seaside suburb on a bright, summer day. In 1973 two young girls, 11-year-old Joanne Ratcliff and 4-year-old Kirstie Gordon disappeared from the Adelaide Oval during an Aussie Rules football match. None of these children has been seen since, but they will never be forgotten and the police files are still open.

The very beginning

The preliminary hearings of the 'Truro Murders' began in September 1979 and concerned seven young women, including 16-year-old Juliet Mykyta, who had been abducted and murdered two years earlier. They were found buried near Truro, a mid-north country town. The other horrific event was the iron-ically named 'Family Murders' which began in June 1979 with the death of teenager Alan Barnes on his 17th birthday.

A short time earlier, Ray Whitrod, the recently retired Police Com-missioner in Queensland (1970–76) attended a meeting of the retired teachers group where Ray Kidney, the Director of OARS (Offenders Aid and Rehabilitation Services of South Australia Incorporated) was the guest speaker. OARS is an organisation which supports discharged criminals and their families. Their services include counselling, pre-release programs and post-release accommodation if needed.

Ray Kidney was discussing the rehabilitation of prisoners, when a woman from the audience enquired about what was being done for the victims: The response was not a lot, but that there was certainly a need.

'Not being one to sit back quietly', as he wrote later, Ray then stood up and suggested that victims *also* needed a supportive organisation. After further discussion, those present decided that a public action group meeting would be held in the near future, sponsored by members of the Flinders Street Baptist Church.

The meeting was the subject of an article in *The Advertiser* written by journalist Stewart Cockburn. Judy Barnes read the article and rang Anne-Marie Mykyta; subsequently, they both rang Ray Whitrod and asked him to help them form a support group for victims. 'Not me, I'm going fishing. But Anne-Marie had a powerful personality and she wasn't accepting this sort of cop-out', he recorded.

The Reverend Barrie Hibbert, then Minister of the Flinders Street Baptist Church in Adelaide, describes how he became involved. Ray Whitrod was a member of his congregation and what follows is an extract from Barrie's interview. He was referring to Sunday, 19 August 1979.

> I AM TENTATIVELY ENGAGED IN PLANNING FOR A NEW CHRISTIAN COMMUNITY SERVICE — POSSIBLY CALLED THE SAMARITAN INSTITUTE
>
> A VOLUNTARY NON-POLITICAL ORGANIZATION OF CONCERNED CITIZENS INTERESTED IN THE WELFARE OF VICTIMS OF CRIME —
>
> ITS VERY EARLY IN MY THINKING BUT "THE ADVERTISER" GIVES ITS BLESSING (SEE MONDAY & TUESDAY'S ISSUES) —
>
> I'LL NEED CHRISTIAN SUPPORT — PERHAPS A CHRISTIAN SHARING FELLOWSHIP MEETING FOR CREKKER?

**Original note from
Ray Whitrod**

Ray and I hit it off immediately – he is just a very, very interesting character. He had only just come back to Adelaide having had all of his trials and tribulations up in Queensland. Then one Sunday morning I noticed Ray scribbling, sitting in the pew there while I was preaching … and on his way out of Church, he handed me this note. 'I've got an idea about victims of serious crime and sort of based on the story of the Good Samaritan – and I'd like to talk to you about it.' And that was it.

The following week a meeting took place after the Sunday service, in the kitchen of the Flinders Street Baptist Church. Present were Ray Whitrod, Barrie, Ray Kidney, John Halsey and Richard Huxter and discussion took place on how to advance the idea of victim support.

The inaugural meeting

This led to an informal meeting of the Truro parents and others who had suffered in similar circumstances, which was held in Ray and Mavis Whitrod's home on 11 October 1979, accompanied by tea and coffee, cakes and scones. The immediate aims were:

- The introduction of the right of the Crown to appeal in those cases where the punishment was regarded as inadequate

- The abolition of the privilege of the unsworn statement

- End the secrecy of parole releases

- Improve compensation claim procedures

- Arrange for better court arrangements for victims

- Publicise VOCS (Victims of Crime Service)

- Recruit 100 members

- Offer support to Truro and other victimised parents

- Be self-sufficient.

The Attorney-General at the time, Chris Sumner, welcomed the proposal and offered assistance. He was approached to discuss ways of implementing the aims of the new VOCS organisation. Soon after that meeting, however, the government changed. The new Attorney-General, Trevor Griffin, also proved sympathetic but the offer of help from the government was not taken up initially except for the use of spare office space at a nominal rent. The early decision not to have paid office staff was based on the fact that Crisis Care, which had been operating since 1976 and was funded by the government, provided a 24-hour service for short-term intervention. VSS, on the other hand, aimed to provide support for

Ray and Mavis Whitrod

longer periods and a more personal service for victims, based on friendship and a firm desire to stay independent of government and rely on volunteers.

Those present at the very first meeting articulated their deep dissatisfaction with the criminal justice system. Consequently, and in order to address the perceived inadequacies and injustices of the system, the South Australian Victim of Crime Service (VOCS) was established in an office in Mead Hall, 65 Flinders Street, adjacent to the Baptist Church, on 16 October 1979. The Reverend Barrie Hibbert eventually became Chairman of VOCS and was associated with the organisation for approximately seven-and-half years before he left to work in London in 1987.

Little had been done to help victims in the ten years prior to these events but what had been achieved to that time provided a solid enough foundation on which to build. The Criminal Injuries Compensation scheme was introduced in 1969 with payments up to $1000. In 1970 several women's shelters were opened, and the Sexual Assault Clinic at the Queen Elizabeth Hospital was established. Legislation for rape reform which gave greater acknowledgment of victims' rights was enacted in 1976.

In his retirement to Adelaide Ray Whitrod brought with him a pioneering reformist reputation, having successfully introduced change into the conservative Queensland police culture during 1970–76. This included an all-female interviewing team for rape victims and the employment of more women police, steps which were considered radical at the time. However, persistent interference from the Queensland Government, which also turned a blind eye when corrupt police were promoted despite objections from Ray, eventually convinced him that it was time to move on. The final straw was the Premier's insistence that Terence Lewis be appointed Assistant Commissioner. Thirteen years later following the Fitzgerald Inquiry into Corruption, Lewis was jailed for 14 years. Ray's legacy to Queensland was that many of the reforms he had attempted without success are now part of the policing culture in that state and across Australia.

In the beginning a group of parents who had lost children in tragic and gruesome circumstances approached Ray Whitrod for advice and assistance in providing support for victims of crime. The bereaved parents could not have found a more capable leader to establish the new organisation in the face of public ignorance and indifference. His energy, skills, knowledge and determination were outstanding.

For many years Ray Whitrod seemed to be all things to all people at VSS.

Court Companion, fund-raiser, public speaker recruiting members from all around the state, and petitioner to government departments for support and recognition.

In a newsletter in which he expressed his admiration for members who would drop everything to visit someone in a crisis Ray wrote:

> It's just as well that everybody is not like me, full of good intentions, but very anxious to postpone any personal inconvenience.

With his wry, self-deprecating humour he was doing himself an injustice, since his willingness to help anyone in need set the example which others followed. Ray never seemed to be off duty or need holidays and was always available by phone, day and night, to those who required his assistance. His commitment attracted and motivated new volunteers to the service.

Twenty years later and busy writing, Ray was still receiving mail and visits from people he had helped and inspired.

Eileen

Eileen, a sprightly and highly articulate woman in her mid-70s, stands in the dock and in a clear and determined voice reads her victim impact statement to the Court.

Some months prior to the hearing, Eileen's purse had been stolen while she was shopping in the local supermarket. She had noticed a nice-looking young man wandering around the shelves without selecting any items and wondered if he was short of money, although he seemed well-dressed, well, tidy anyway, she thought.

Then while she was trying to make up her mind which cheese she fancied, her shopping trolley was pushed hard against her legs, nearly knocking her over. Turning, she realised the attacker – the young man she had noticed earlier – was running down the aisle with her bag, and she began shouting for someone to stop him.

A young couple who looked like ordinary shoppers but turned out to be store detectives converged at the checkout and caught the offender.

The young man whose name was Ian was taken to the manager's office, police were called and he was arrested. Later Eileen learned that Ian had a drug problem but had expressed remorse for his actions. Nevertheless, with the supportive presence of a Court Companion Eileen was determined to pursue the matter, stating that she wished to make a stand for all elderly people, particularly women, who had their bags stolen, especially where the offenders had not been caught.

In her statement, Eileen described the severe bruising she had suffered and the fright she'd had, making it difficult for her to return to her nearest supermarket. Ian lowered his head and formally apologised to Eileen for his actions through his Counsel. She could see he seemed genuinely upset and she thought of her own grandson who was also in his early twenties.

When asked by the Judge for her comments, Eileen again stood up and said that she accepted Ian's apology and felt that she could forgive him. The young man had tears in his eyes and could only nod when he was ordered to compensate Eileen for her loss, at the same time being warned that a repeat performance could land him in jail.

Defending Counsel and the magistrate commended Eileen for her thoughtful attitude. Outside the court she told her Court Companion that now that she was no longer angry she felt better knowing Ian would not go to jail.

Ray Whitrod, full of enthusiasm and zest for life, with a wide experience in four different police forces, was never going to be content to just play golf or go fishing. Instead, he made a lasting impression on Australia, and South Australia in particular, and his name will always be linked to the development of victims' rights and the establishment of the now re-named, Victim Support Service.

The organisation was up and running with a sense of urgency and an immense dynamism which would exhaust some of the people involved. The costs were high but the benefits to the community in the past and the future are immeasurable.

So who were these amazing people?

2. The pioneers

The young sow wild oats.
The old grow sage.

Sir Winston Churchill

It is usual for exciting stories to have a hero or heroine and this story is full of them. Pioneers are special people who see a need or opportunity and open it up for others to follow.

Australian communities, and particularly that of South Australia, owe a great debt to the vision and tenacity of the people who started VSS. In a short overview it is impossible to mention everyone who has ever made a contribution, but many of the early pioneers demonstrated outstanding commitment to the organisation. We are fortunate to have others like them today, people who are motivating, inspiring and generous with their time and effort.

The early days were very difficult for the organisation, as it attempted to persuade both the government and the community to accept a new concept and to raise the money to fund it. The methodology was simple. It consisted of endless talking, persistent argument and using every opportunity for ethical advertising.

For those involved, the punishing schedule in the first few months included reports to the media, both in Australia and New Zealand, speaking on more than 40 occasions about the organisation to a diversity of groups, and letters to the government and various members of parliament. The result was a tally of 700 members in South Australia and some funds in the kitty. A party was held to encourage the Truro parents and others. The initial schedule was so demanding that it was feared that burnout and health problems would become an issue.

As the profile of VSS expanded, there were increasing referrals from the police and approaches from victims of crime. Contact with victims varied in intensity, depending on their needs, and could include visiting a critically injured person in hospital two or three times a week or referring another to VSS's legal adviser. A number of people reported that they had tried every possible avenue for help and the new organisation was their last resort.

Ray Whitrod

In this environment Ray Whitrod made a huge impact. All the early reports and those interviewed acknowledge that, without Ray's incredible determination, VSS may not have got off the ground, let alone still be alive and kicking hard.

Ray was the first executive officer. In his long and varied career he had developed high-level connections in governments and in the public service which he did not hesitate to call upon. He was a multi-skilled human dynamo focused on problem-solving. He is remembered for his compassion and ready laugh – and equally his impatience when things did not turn out well. He often referred to himself as grouchy.

In a 1981 newsletter Ray wrote:

I must admit ashamedly that I have a weakness for confrontation rather than compromise (sometimes called conciliation) only because I am too impatient! You all will know that conciliation is by far the most rewarding because it is true that nobody is ever convinced by an argument.

Later when discussing the need for frequent negotiation on behalf of VSS he explained:

I'm afraid I've been too long a servant of the Queen to want to work too far outside the system; not in the sense of defying it, but I would rather seek cooperation from all the powers that be.

Following Ray's resignation as Chairman of VOCS at the end of 1991, Bob Whitington, a former journalist and long-time friend, described Ray's career in a VSS newsletter article from which the following facts are extracted.

Ray Wells Whitrod, AC, CVO, QPM, MA, BEc, Dip. Criminology (Cambridge) was born in the West End of Adelaide in 1916 and attended the Adelaide Boys High School. In 1934 he joined the South Australian Police as a cadet constable and was attached to the Criminal Investigation Branch (CIB) from 1941–45. During the Second World War he joined the RAAF and was attached to the RAF Coastal Command in England, attaining the rank of Flight Lieutenant.

After the war Ray rejoined the CIB in Adelaide before leaving in 1949 to join the Australian Security Intelligence Organisation (ASIO) in Sydney where he became Assistant Director. From there he took up the position of Director of the Commonwealth Investigation Service in 1953 at the age of 36.

In 1960 Ray became the first Commissioner of the Commonwealth Police Force, the establishment of which he had recommended to the federal government. In 1969 he was appointed Commissioner of the Papua-New Guinea Constabulary and in 1970 he became Commissioner of the Queensland Police Force from which, as noted earlier, he retired in 1976. In 1971 he was named Queenslander of the Year.

In the late 1960s Ray studied criminology at Cambridge University having already achieved a Master of Arts and Bachelor of Economics. Following retirement, he was Visiting Fellow at the Australian National University between 1977–78 where he undertook a research project on fear at the Australian Institute of Criminology, in addition to some lecturing. The university awarded him an Honorary Doctorate of Laws.

Other distinctions included his being the only Australian policeman to be awarded the Queen's Gold Medal for an essay on juvenile delinquency in a competition conducted in 1965 by the British Foreign Office. Ray was a Life Member of the South Australian Scouts. He was also the only Australian policeman to win the Sir George Murray award for the best published article on public administration (in 1977) and the only Australian to deliver the Sir John Barry Memorial Lecture at Melbourne University.

Ray established the Australasian Society of Victimology in 1987, the year the Victimology Course commenced in South Australia, with Ray and Harold Weir as invited lecturers. The current CEO of VSS continues to provide input into this course. Ray was a founding member of the World Society of Victimology and served on its executive. In 1990 he was awarded the Advance Australia award for Community Service.

A man of many parts, in 1983 he ran the Gawler-to-Adelaide marathon (approximately 50 km) in five hours at the age of 68, and later blamed his arthritic hips on that stupendous effort! There seemed nothing he could not achieve once he set his mind to it.

Ray had several bouts of ill health and hospitalisation for surgery, and in 1989, he withdrew as Executive Director. Subsequently, VSS advertised this as a paid position. He was appointed Chairman of the Council, and following his resignation from VSS, became its first and so far, only Patron. In 1993 Ray Whitrod was awarded a Companion of the Order of Australia (AC) in the Australia Day Honours List.

Ray died in 2003.

Judith Barnes

While Judy never became very involved with the organisational side of VSS, she was there at the early meetings and always available to help anyone referred to her either by the police or VSS. In her interview Judy says she preferred to remain independent in her activities, protesting about shortcomings in the justice system, writing letters to governments and generally speaking out whenever she had an opportunity. At the same time she wished to avoid attracting media attention if there was an issue over which she and VSS were at odds. 'I might want to chain myself to the Attorney-General's desk', she said.

At the same time Judy and her family were fighting their own battles over son Alan's death and it took eleven long years before their last court appearance. The family suffered a wide and ongoing range of post-traumatic stress problems, some of which are unresolved to this day.

For many years Judy and her daughter Cherie have contributed to courses on victimology at TAFE and through the Police Education Unit. Without flinching they re-tell in plain terms the effect the brutal crime has had on their family, while emphasising their opposition to the death penalty.

Judy says she is not afraid of telling the truth, only afraid of lies. She marvels that her friend Anne-Marie Mykyta was able to forgive her daughter's killer – 'That shows you the calibre of the woman'. Judy adds that she couldn't do that. Yet she shows comparable courage and integrity in continuing to put herself on the line in the interests of other victims of crime.

John Halsey

John Halsey

John was an old acquaintance of Ray's from the Flinders Street Baptist Church whom he knew from the study groups which were held at that time. He has a background in education and public policy which made him eminently suitable for Ray's early recruiting drive in 1979.

John was a member of Council for many years, including the period in 1995 when VSS was experiencing difficulties. He had been a member of the selection committee which had appointed Andrew Paterson as CEO and recalled that period had also been difficult, like 'a snake shedding an old skin'. He presided over changed premises, balancing staffing with volunteers and the VSS's increasing reliance on government funding. John saw Ray's desire to 'keep Government at arm's length' as a result of his painful experience with the Queensland Government during his time there as Commissioner of Police.

John believed the 1995–96 review of VSS had been necessary and established the organisation on a sound footing for the future. He closed his interview with the following words in referring to the development of VSS: 'If you have a good idea, pursue it, because we need good ideas in society to continue to build the fabric and the infrastructure to support people'.

In recognition of his length of service John was made a Life Member of VSS when he retired.

Barrie Hibbert

The Reverend Barrie Hibbert, an early recruit to VSS, became its first Chairman, supporting Ray as Executive Director. His Baptist Church facilities gave the new organisation its first premises with their use of the office above the Church Hall.

Barrie derived great satisfaction in problem-solving with Ray, being part of an interesting group of individuals and in the knowledge he was doing something

Barrie Hibbert

worthwhile to help those who had suffered so severely. He also enjoyed the social interaction afforded by membership of the group.

In 2003 he conducted the funeral of his old friend Ray Whitrod which was a colourful and memorable service.

Rosemary and Richard Huxter

Rosemary and Richard were two of the founding members of VSS and Richard was present at the first informal meeting in the kitchen of the Flinders Street Baptist Church Hall. While working as an industrial officer, he wrote the organisation's first constitution and continued to provide support behind the scenes.

Rosemary Huxter

Rosemary

Following her retirement in 1999 Ray Whitrod referred to her as: 'Our first house mother, the mainstay of the operation'. Rosemary answered a call for help from Ray in 1987 for administration assistance. Commonwealth funding had run out and the office activities needed coordinating.

The timing was perfect as the last of the five Huxter offspring had just matriculated and Rosemary was considering rejoining the workforce.

She loved working at Victim Support Service, a place 'where you could make a difference'. Rosemary has never been a victim of crime, but doesn't believe that it could never happen to her. Her attitude is: 'There, but for the grace of God, go I'.

Rosemary started working five days a week from 9 am to 1 pm and she was the face of Victim Support Service for twelve months until new funding enabled the agency to take on additional staff. She stayed for twelve years and her job evolved into that of Office Manager – she was someone who understood every aspect of the organisation.

When she left, CEO Andrew Paterson, wrote, 'My abiding image is of Rosemary in full flight, getting the job done with attention to detail and a deep and abiding concern for people'. David Kerr remembers her commitment and attitude to 'getting on with it'. Whether it was staying back to take Council minutes, organising annual general meetings, coordinating volunteers or collating newsletters, she would do it cheerfully and without fuss. Rosemary masterminded the move from King William Street to Halifax Street and arranged delicious food for any occasion; nothing was too much trouble. Ray Whitrod, describing the early days in Flinders Street wrote:

> Rosemary provided backroom support of the highest order. Our paperwork was kept to a minimum; the occasional caller was given immediate attention and made welcome. Since many of our members were folk we had recruited in the country areas, their infrequent contact with our service was important to them, and Rosemary ensured the office was clean and tidy and frugal. She somehow managed to strengthen their feelings of doing something worthwhile in belonging to us.

The name, Rosemary Huxter, is synonymous with the early history of Victim Support Service and her phenomenal memory for detail continues to be an asset.

Anne-Marie Mykyta

Anne-Marie was a well-known Adelaide playwright and author who came to greater public attention in 1977 when her 16-year-old daughter, Juliet, became one of the Truro murder victims. Anne-Marie showed exceptional fortitude, and with Judy Barnes, approached Ray Whitrod, who had been featured in the press as a person who believed more should be done for victims of crime. They persuaded him to help them to establish an organisation, which concentrated on the needs of victims.

Anne-Marie and Myk Mykyta

Anne-Marie and her husband Irush ('Myk') were present at the first meeting at the Whitrods' home. In his interview Myk describes himself as 'an adjunct to Anne-Marie's passionate involvement' in VSS, but he has served on the Board and written articles for VSS. Latterly he has offered service as a judge of the Mitchell Media awards.

Myk's impression of that first meeting was that because the participants were so immersed in their own problems that only Ray could make VSS happen. Anne-Marie's driving aim was to give the support to others she had needed during the Truro Trial.

In her book, *It's a Long Way to Truro*, Anne-Marie describes in graphic detail the pain of losing a child, the two years before Juliet was found and the struggle to simply function as a family during the long drawn-out legal processes. Anne-Marie was a strong, direct and colourful personality who, in spite of her own agony, was always willing to help others, day or night.

In 1979 Anne-Marie received a phone call from Judy Barnes, who was experiencing desperation after Alan's death because no one seemed to understand what she was going through. Feeling suicidal, she rang Anne-Marie after seeing her photo in the paper. Judy begged: 'Don't hang up, don't hang up!' 'I'm not going to hang up', Anne-Marie replied and they talked for four hours. Later, Judy flushed away the prescribed tablets she had been stockpiling. Judy says in her interview that, although in many ways, they were absolute opposites, she and Anne-Marie formed an unbreakable bond and from that time on, they were always there for one another.

Following the Truro murders' four-week trial in February 1980, James Miller was sentenced to life in prison for his part in the murders where he acted as chauffeur in picking up young women. The prosecution claimed that, after the first crime, he failed to intervene when he had the opportunity, although he knew what was happening. Miller had been a close friend of Christopher Worrell, a good-looking man half his age, whom he had met in jail and who was the primary perpetrator of the crimes.

According to an Australian study, 50 per cent of murderers of young women have previous convictions for sexual assault. And so it was in this case. Worrell, aged 23, had been free on early parole from a sentence of six years for two cases involving attempted rape and indecent assault. On his release he embarked upon a ferocious killing spree lasting 51 days during which time the seven young women disappeared. The murders stopped with his death in a car accident which also killed a female passenger and slightly injured Miller. Worrell therefore, did not live to be charged.

Anne-Marie returned to teaching, but eventually retired in 1981 to concentrate on writing, teaching workshops and talking and listening to other people. She taught girls at the Magill Remand Centre and received remarkable poems and letters of appreciation from many students. Some of them were people whom others had labelled illiterate or incorrigible. In 1995 Anne-Marie met James Miller in prison and said later that she had forgiven him.

Anne-Marie died in 1996 having devoted an extraordinary amount of effort over the intervening years to assisting other victims of crime. For 11 years she made a huge contribution to VSS, including a period on Council as Chairperson.

Anne-Marie kept her sense of humour to the end, quoting in a letter to her friends, words from *Carmen*: 'I have merely gone ahead. I'll grab a good table, order some good wine and watch the dancers until the rest of you catch up with me'. She was only 56 and a very special person who will never be forgotten by those who were privileged to meet her.

> *How does it feel when your life falls apart?*
> *When your dreams have all gone astray?*
> *When you waken each morn and can't make a start?*
> *You're unsure if you'll get through the day.*

First verse of *Chrysalis*

Debra S 1998

Ron Penglase

Ray gave a talk to the Naval and Military Club in 1986, which Ron found impressive. During his talk Ray asked for someone to take over the accounts at VSS and Ron volunteered as Treasurer. In those days the accounting system was fairly simple and Ron attended two or three days a week to pay bills and dispense pay cheques. He held this position until 1997 during which time the finances had become more complex and Ron introduced computing into the office, initially using his own machine. He is quoted as remarking in the early days:

Ron Penglase

VOCS is an organisation filled with such stories of courage and fortitude they could double the sales of any supermarket magazine.

Molly Reilly

Molly was one of Ray's right-hand helpers in the early years, remembered by many of the early staff. She was a volunteer who 'buzzed around the office like a bluebottle fly', especially when it came to getting the newsletter out on time and keeping membership information up to date. In 1988 as a mark of appreciation Molly was made an Honorary Life Member of VSS.

Harold Weir

Harold Weir

Harold is a multi-talented member of VSS and had already experienced a full and varied career before he joined the organisation in 1987. At different times he had been a Congregational Minister, an accountant, a psychologist, prison worker, criminologist and saw active service in the RAAF. He is an author, was very involved in the Prisoners' Aid Association, and at one time was the World President of the International Prisoners' Aid Association.

He worked for the United Nations in Japan and as a federal librarian in Canberra; he started the Justice Administration Program at the former South Australian Institute of Technology, now the University of South Australia. Somewhere in this amazing career he found time to write South Australia's first manual on victimology.

Invited by Ray to join the VSS Council in 1987, he eventually became Chairman when Ray became ill, and took leave of absence from other activities in July of that year. Harold found himself running VSS at the time when a group of volunteers resigned en masse. They had been attempting unsuccessfully for some time to persuade the hierarchy that they needed professional social work assistance to handle really difficult cases. Harold was sympathetic and managed to obtain enough funding to appoint social workers Kate Hannaford and Jan McClelland for twelve months. In January 1988 he was also instrumental in bringing Des House on board as administrative assistant. On his return, Ray was not enthusiastic about the changes.

During an interview in 1999 Harold describes the difficulty in persuading some of the Council members that these changes had been necessary. He recalls a meeting which became very heated and Harold was afraid Bob Whitington was going to have a heart attack. He said: 'Now listen here Bob, don't use me as an excuse to have a heart attack, you have your own heart attack'. Harold's gentle humour helped to calm things down.

Harold is still convinced that the only way for VSS to meet the strong demand for the range of services it supplies, is for professional staff and volunteers to work together and he is thrilled by the cooperative system currently operating.

Harold left in October 1988 when Ray was back in the driving seat. His active period in VSS as Chairman and virtually CEO, lasted only 15 months but in that short time he ushered in what he described as 'a sea change which was pretty drastic' and which has never been reversed. Both Harold and Ray continued to provide lectures on victimology to police and other professionals at the University of South Australia for several years.

Bob Whitington

Bob Whitington

Bob was a renowned journalist who had spent many years as the senior crime reporter on the local South Australian paper, The Advertiser, which he had joined as a cub reporter in 1935. He retired in 1982 and joined VSS's Media Committee. He was a great admirer and confidant of Ray and became his primary assistant in the public speaking circuit. Part of their camaraderie stemmed from the fact that both served in the Australian Air Force during the Second World War, although Bob was unfortunate enough to have been a prisoner of the Japanese for three-and-half years.

Bob was a Council member for nine years, and between 1989 and 1993, he was editor of the VOCS newsletter. He was awarded an Honorary Life Membership of VSS in 1988 in appreciation of his work. Bob's background and contacts with media people were often a bonus for VSS when press reports needed correction or information needed to be conveyed to journalists.

To Anne-Marie Mykyta and many others he was an invaluable and very special friend. To Judith Barnes he was a 'second father'. To another victim he was Uncle Bob. Throughout the long period of searching for the missing Truro victims, the trial and for many years afterwards, he was always available for support, advising victims how to handle the media, listening and comforting, more like a family friend than an investigative journalist.

When Bob Whitington died in May 1996, Anne-Marie wrote a deeply felt tribute to his strength and caring attitude which had helped to support so many victims of crime. Sadly she was to lose her own battle with illness five months later.

Government supporters

This seems an appropriate place to acknowledge two outstanding champions of victims of crime. As Attorneys-General in opposing political parties, they were both strong and consistent supporters of VSS for more than 22 years, whether in government or opposition.

Victims in South Australia and beyond owe a great deal to these two very able and approachable Attorneys-General who, while in office, possessed the integrity and commitment to make far-reaching changes for the benefit of society. Both Trevor Griffin and Chris Sumner frequently attended VSS special events and annual general meeting's together – a generous gesture.

Christopher Sumner

Christopher Sumner

Chris, as everyone calls him, graduated from Adelaide University with degrees in law and arts. He entered politics in 1975 and was South Australia's Attorney-General for a short period in 1979 until there was a change of government. When a Labor Government was returned in 1982, he resumed that role until his retirement from Parliament in 1994, becoming the longest serving Attorney-General in South Australia's history. He is a member of the World Society of Victimology (President from 1991 to 1994) and is currently the President of the Australasian Society of Victimology.

Among his many achievements was the major role he played in having a Declaration on the Rights of Victims of Crime accepted by the 7th United Nations Congress on Crime Prevention held in Milan in 1985. Many preliminary meetings were required, some of which involved Ray Whitrod. Defining the word 'victim' to suit various countries met with opposition and some difficulties. However, the final draft was passed just before the deadline by dividing it into two parts. Part A referred to victims of crime and their treatment in the criminal justice system, and Part B referred to victims of abuse of power.

The declaration was subsequently endorsed by the United Nations General Assembly in December 1985 and later implemented by the South Australian Government in that year – another first for South Australia.

Chris Sumner's door was always open to Ray Whitrod, and their good professional relationship, which combined friendship with mutual respect, led to many positive outcomes for victims of crime.

Trevor Griffin

Trevor graduated from Adelaide University with bachelor and masters degrees in law. He was a member of the Liberal Government in 1978 and served as Attorney-General from 1979 to 1982 and again from 1993 to 2001. Like his political counterpart, whether in government or opposition, he had an abiding concern for victims of crime – expressed through improved funding for VSS and amending or developing appropriate legislation.

Trevor Griffin

Trevor requested and assisted in the expansion of VSS to five regional areas, and in 1999, initiated the Victims of Crime Review, which led to the *Victims of Crime Act*, promulgated in 2001 and implemented in 2003. He always consulted closely with VSS when appropriate in relation to activities, events, financing and legislative change. Even though they might not always have agreed, Trevor reports that it was a close relationship.

* * * *

These have been brief sketches of just a few of the people who have provided loyal and consistent support over the years; other pioneers are mentioned throughout the book. We still need, and are fortunate to have, pioneers like these.

Now you may be wondering what turns a victim into a volunteer?

3. Victim to volunteer

Volunteers are not paid; not because they are worthless but because they are priceless.

Anon.

While it has never been necessary for volunteers working at VSS to be survivors of crime, Ray Whitrod had a soft spot for victims who expressed their appreciation for the support and counselling they had received by offering their services at a later stage of their recovery. Not everyone is able or inclined to respond in this way, but up to and including the present, a number of the volunteer staff have been victims.

The aims of the service as described in the report reviewing the first three years, can be stated concisely as 'support and advocacy for victims of crime', and include the primary victims and those who are financially or psychologically dependent on them. Victims also include those who are inconvenienced by crime, as well as taxpayers, insurers and consumers who pay higher charges as the result of the crime cost component.

The *Macquarie Concise Dictionary* defines victim as 'a sufferer from any destructive, injurious or adverse action or agency'. A victim of crime attracts a wider definition depending on the crime. In 1988 Ray attended and reported on an international conference in Melbourne, 'Dealing with Stress and Trauma in Emergency Services', which included a paper by Professor Tony Taylor from New Zealand. He postulated six very comprehensive classifications of victims as follows:

1. The primary victim who has actual involvement with the perpetrator

2. The secondary victim who can be family, friend or flatmate etc.

3. The tertiary victims who are those in official positions, for example, police, lawyers, judges and correctional officers

4. People in the community who identify with the people involved

5. Those in the community who are emotionally immature and are stimulated by sensational media coverage

6. The witnesses of the offence who are required to remember details for later cross-examination or sit on a jury to hear evidence and then return a verdict which leads to a penalty.

A graphic account of a crime read in the newspaper can bury itself in a vulnerable subconscious to be recalled when memory is nudged. An example is the elderly woman, Helene, who as a young woman in Europe burst into tears on reading the story of a girl raped and murdered on a bombsite after the Second World War. The only clue to her identity was a smart red shoe. The picture it generated in Helene's mind seemed so sad and pitiful. For years, the sight of a red fashion shoe would bring tears to her eyes.

More serious, but just as persistent in its long-term effect, is Ray's story of the Adelaide wife who joined VSS after armed robbers held up her husband twice in their post office. She described how her husband looks up with apprehension every time someone enters the shop. He has nightmares and other long-term problems associated with a life-threatening experience. Both of them feel depressed. How could volunteers assist them?

The early vision of VOCS was a 'Volunteer Offering Care' whose role was to:

> To help people, care for people, to encourage or support people who have been or are the victims of crime.

The aim was to provide support for recent victims by 'offering the friendship of a similar sufferer'. The main emphasis at that time was that victims could best be helped by other people who had been victimised in a similar way. Ray referred often to Anne-Marie Mykyta and Judy Barnes who supported each other by sharing their sorrow in facing a bleak future without a beloved child and then went on to help others who had suffered in the same way. Ray wrote: 'In establishing a good rapport, an earlier victim has a head start on a complete outsider – at least that's my experience with victims'.

To a great extent this is true and is the basis of the support groups which are set up by VSS. This philosophy was considered important with regard to Court Companions (refer chapter 6) but is less significant when it comes to general membership and the helpers who were desperately needed to undertake the many office and administration tasks requiring volunteers.

In November 1979 Ray released a general letter to explain the formation of VOCS and enclosed a brochure. He began with the comment:

> If you are concerned about the amount of today's crime, uncertain as to the adequacy of judicial penalties, dismayed at the absence of offenders' remorse and the lack of the restitution of stolen property, worried at the possibility that your home, shop or factory may be broken into next, anxious at the expansion of drug abuse in this country, this letter should interest you.

Then he went on to describe the aims of VSS and to invite the reader to become a member, listing the membership fees of $5 for a family and $3 for a pensioner.

Caren

Seated in the Supreme Court, Caren sobbed quietly while listening to the evidence of the Forensic Pathologist. The exhaustive details of the horrific injuries suffered by her brother, Ken, during his brutal and savage murder, were in the end, too much for her and she and her Court Companion left the courtroom.

They were a close family and she had loved her brother, he was her best friend. Almost three years older than her, he had always been protective, escorting her to and from school and later picking her up from parties when she became a teenager. Her father used to joke that Ken sometimes made him feel superfluous, but in reality, the family was very proud of their hard-working son who cared so much for his two younger sisters.

Caren is a strong and brave person, and each day she returned to the trial to endure the agony of hearing evidence. She felt it was the least she could do for her adored brother who had been beaten to death without reason, especially since neither of their parents could stand the pain of being in court. Her sister stayed at home to support them. At night over dinner Caren would interpret the evidence in as gentle a way as possible and then fall into bed exhausted, only to lie awake for hours, as words and phrases from the day continued to run through her mind.

Finally Caren had the satisfaction of hearing the offender being found guilty and sentenced to a lengthy non-parole period. She knew then what other victims meant when they were quoted in the media as saying, 'We have been given a life sentence – one day the culprit will be free'. Fifteen years down the track that ghastly man will be walking the streets again, but nothing would bring Ken back.

Prior to the trial Caren had sought help from Victim Support Service and subsequently joined the 'Moving Forward Women's Group'. This involvement gave her a sense of balance and brought issues into perspective. She found that sharing problems and receiving support for post-trial ill-health, really did help her to come to terms with her loss, and in time she was able to assist her parents.

Although she admits she was at first sceptical, Caren is eternally grateful for the help that she and her family were given by the Victim Support Service during that terrible time, especially by her Court Companion whose strength and understanding never faltered.

Traumatic stress

People often underestimate the trauma, fear, loss of power and the lack of understanding that Caren and other victims encounter. The physical and psychological reactions to becoming a victim are well documented as responses to severe stress. They include headaches, shaking, crying, sadness and feelings of isolation. In addition, there may be a loss of trust, flashbacks, panic attacks, nightmares and sleeping problems.

Victims are sometimes blamed for their plight, which adds greatly to their distress. Comments about wearing provocative clothing, the media sensationalising aspects of the crime, the feelings of helpless fragility and a fear of the legal system all amount to secondary victimisation.

Not so well documented are the many and varied ways in which some victims are often re-victimised. Constantly seeing a picture of your murdered child in the media is bad enough but the shock of realising that it was taken after death, even though you had supplied a recent photo to the authorities is an agonising experience.

Threatening phone calls and pets killed on your property are just as frightening as the stranger who calls at your home 'to meet the murder family'. Dealing with members of the media who, having climbed tall back fences only to be rebuffed, then slap advertising stickers on your car, which lift paint when removed, are beneath contempt. Nevertheless, such incidents are deeply disturbing to the victims of the crime. Then there is the loss of 'friends', who don't want to be involved, the neighbours who cross to the other side of the street – the list goes on.

For the sake of balance the positive experiences also need mention. Although they tend to be fewer, the effects may last longer. The neighbours who, unasked, supply meals and the strangers who hug you in the street and whisper 'Good luck'. The small, anonymous posies left at your front door each day you are in court, and the police and counsellors who go out of their way to provide support. Human nature is a strange mixture.

What do victims need?

Victims need some or all of the following to regain their sense of self. They need to be believed and acknowledged, not blamed. Compassionate listening is essential, asking 'Are you OK?' and meaning it. Police need to keep the victim informed of the progress of the investigation.

Don't be over-protective but ask people if they want to talk? Some days they might, other days not. Help with small chores and offer to accompany them to appointments, as going out alone may be a problem for a while.

Last, but not least, *don't* tell them it's time they got over it, and *never* compare their experiences with your own.

Recovery from trauma

In the February 1984 newsletter Anne-Marie Mykyta describes in some detail the physical effects she suffered as the result of extreme stress. She drank more heavily and desperately, stopped exercising, depended on sleeping pills and couldn't be bothered to eat properly.

The major problem was overwhelming fatigue, and eventually Anne-Marie tried a variety of vitamin and mineral supplements and raw juices. In addition, she listened to soothing music, had hot milk at bedtime and meditated when she had time. Anne-Marie read widely on ways of achieving a sense of acceptance and physical and mental calm. She felt that frustrated anger and guilt, if not talked out, were very self-destructive, and men in particular, were prone to this type of ongoing stress. She planned to start some classes for men to address these issues.

Recovering from severe psychic trauma is a very individual experience and should never be judged. Studies have shown that people who recover from crime most successfully in the long term usually have a positive attitude to life, good relationships and are able to pick up their interrupted goals – although one victim has commented: 'You never get over it. Time just softens the scars'.

Caren too, has moved forward from the crime which devastated her life but to this day, in her endeavour to cope with the traumatic, unnecessary life-changing event, still reflects on the many unanswered questions. The pain has affected and damaged many other lives too, although within her own family it has strengthened the supporting bonds, a situation which doesn't always occur. A year or so after the trial Caren felt strong enough to approach the Victim Support Service to offer some of her spare time as a volunteer to help other victims.

An article in the *Weekend Australian* on 9 August 2003 equates volunteering with improved health in retirement. It also states that people over 55 provide more than a third of the voluntary hours worked in Australia, so it would seem that volunteer work benefits the giver and the community.

Judi Rea

Judi is another example (and there are many) of a victim who subsequently became a volunteer to help others. In 1992 while she and her husband were overseas, their 17-year-old daughter Kirsty was incinerated in a car crash. The other driver was drunk and unlicensed and charged with 'causing death by dangerous driving'. To the family's complete shock, after a high-profile trial and appeal, he was given a suspended sentence, in spite of a history of driving offences.

Struggling through the maze of legal process and lack of familiarity with the technical jargon, Judi wished there was just one person she could approach for coordinated assistance at such a terrible time. Judi was aware that many others were in similar positions and although receiving support from compassionate friends and VSS, she began to campaign for funding. Her aim was for an independent Road Trauma Support Service to apply 'people power' as she put it. In spite of much effort this did not eventuate so Judi joined FAST – Families Against Senseless Tragedy (refer chapter 12) and devoted her energy to a similar group.

Judi became a public speaker with VSS and in 1997 was elected to the Board of Management (or Council as it was then). She completed four-and-a-half years before ill-health forced her to resign, although still maintaining an interest in VSS.

Ethics

Another important early document was a Code of Ethics for Volunteers. The section on philosophy emphasised that the organisation was a voluntary, non-sectarian, non-political group of concerned citizens. The volunteer could provide support to victims in distress but not engage in 'complicated, problem-solving counselling', which requires trained, professional staff. The section on confidentiality described when not to discuss a case, to communicate freely with your client and to report frequently to your coordinator.

Public speakers

Ray and others gave a substantial number of talks to clubs and organisations. He would appeal to his listeners to join VSS on the spot and he wasn't backward in recruiting helpers for specific tasks at the same time. His talent for persuasion seems exceptional and once people became involved he seemed to generate a high level of loyalty. In some instances it might have been a case of 'If you can't beat them join them', but for many, Ray's vision and energy motivated people to contribute in whatever way they could.

That didn't stop his occasional complaints in the newsletter as the following quote demontrates:

> It pains me to realise that out there we have so many members with a great deal of skill and knowledge about surviving in this world, locked away in their grey cells, and apparently they don't realise just what wealth that is.

Ray could also be generous in his praise of others, often in a teasing way as if to hide his fondness for the person concerned. In 1990 he wrote of his old friend, Brian Hall, who had just been elected to Council and had taken on the Membership Committee:

> There may be a few in South Australia who do not know Brian; they will be just off an international flight. Some of us old airmen are overdue at the salvage dump or worse, but Brian still moves about on

maximum revs every day. He's stoking the fire about an hour before first light and then puts out the runway flares at night.

In fact a large number of very skilled people made a huge effort, some for many years. A wide range of individuals pitched in to contribute in different ways according to their time and ability.

Jean Chinca

Jean, whose parents and sister were murdered 17 years before she approached VSS for help, has become another valued volunteer. Jean considered she had coped with the trauma very well but when the killer escaped while on Christmas leave, the shock returned the pain to the forefront of her life.

Jean Chinca

In her interview Jean remarked: 'The help, understanding, support and friendship I have received have been wonderful, and given me a quality of life I thought I had lost for ever. They [the counsellors] taught me to live with caution, not in fear'. She also commented that when her first social worker left she felt she was losing her security blanket but subsequent staff have proved just as skilled and supportive.

Jean joined the 'Ongoing Women's Group' and is a trained member of the Public Speakers' Group for VSS to 'give back a little for all they have given and done for me'.

Volunteers vs. professionals

An ongoing problem for some of those around Ray, and constantly referred to in his writing, was his passionate belief in the value of volunteers above paid staff. He could be quite outspoken in his views, which were often aired in the newsletters and have been quoted in several chapters. He had a great respect for volunteers, which it could be hypothesised, may have stemmed to some degree from his strong Baptist Church background where community service is considered an integral part of membership.

In one newsletter Ray expresses his views on voluntary groups:

Such groups as ours have been defined as voluntary small group structures for mutual aid and the accomplishment of a specific purpose. They are usually formed by peers who have come together for mutual assistance in satisfying a common need, overcoming a common handicap or life-destructing problem, and bringing about desired personal or social change. The initiators see that their needs are not or cannot be met by existing social institutions. Self-help groups emphasise face-to-face interactions and the assumption of personal responsibility by members.

The basis of personal relationships in voluntary agencies are mutual respect, confidence, hope and unshakeable belief in the possibility of what others might regard as impossible.

One can argue for and against such statements, but the reality is that highly principled voluntary and paid staff are not mutually exclusive although they may approach problems from a different point of view and both groups succumb to occasional errors. A strong team approach is still the ideal model at VSS, one which usually leads to outstanding results.

Harold Weir's view that volunteers are essential to VSS but they must have professional guidance, counselling if necessary, and the ability to refer complicated cases, has prevailed. In recent years there has been a deliberate effort to strengthen this partnership and improve strategies to integrate volunteers.

Despite these early disagreements over the role of volunteers, by the mid-1980s, VSS had evolved into a lively, enthusiastic organisation, albeit working under significant difficulties in terms of finance, accommodation and with limited political influence. VSS was beginning to develop an identity, to which members could respond and feel proud to be participants in the drive for recognition.

Approximately 120 volunteers continue to contribute in many ways, often acquiring new skills in the process. They include roles as Court Companions, public speakers, assistants in regional offices, on the Occupational Health and Safety Committee, in administration, judging media awards, on the newsletter committee, in the payroll and finance team, in the Resource Centre, promoting community awareness, and as members of the Board of Management. Volunteers have established and maintained the website and entered statistical data for many years.

Since 1996 new roles have been developed for volunteers and more formalised systems for their recruitment, management and training introduced. Until this initiative a number of volunteers felt undervalued and needed further support. Volunteers in the country had been left to manage with little or no support.

Job descriptions, selection criteria and commitments are developed between VSS and volunteers. Resource materials and training manuals were introduced. Counselling staff became responsible for managing volunteer programs, members of which appear to appreciate the extra structure and professional approach.

In the regional offices even more flexibility and variety are required. Reception duties and practical assistance with victim impact statements are regularly undertaken.

Tomorrow is Now

We need to change the present
our spirits lift with hope
the task seems overwhelming
and complex in its scope.
With careful, dogged planning
a breakthrough we can see
but the outcomes that we yearn for
depend on you and me.

Anon

4. Growing up

The First Birthday was a bobbydazzler – and it takes something to dazzle a bobby!

Ray Whitrod

Ray Whitrod had a precise plan for his vision of a support system for victims of crime and how he hoped the organisation would develop. He wrote very comprehensive notes for the inaugural meeting entitled 'A Samaritan Institute', which he described as:

> A voluntary, independent, non-political, non-profit making association of concerned citizens organised to promote the welfare of victims of crime, both in general, and in specific circumstances.

Ray went on to outline the possible goals, the professional skills required from constituent volunteers and some organisational models. He discussed budgets, response to the media, staffing – 'we could set out to tap the retired group, the elderly are by far the most responsive' and many other issues. The hand-written six-page document flows into a thoroughly considered proposal, carefully reviewing all the possible options required for speedy implementation.

Before long it was realised that the organisation could not be called Samaritan as that name was already registered elsewhere. The name, 'Volunteers Offering Care' evolved into 'Victims of Crime Service' and so VOCS was born.

The Truro Murder Trials were due to start in September 1979 and those most affected needed an organisation in place to provide guidance and support. The victim families felt desolate, lacking assistance and understanding, so it was appropriate that the main objectives were advocacy, support and reform.

First and foremost VSS represents victims of crime. The second aim was to push for law reform in areas which particularly disadvantaged victims at a time when public opinion seemed to be focus on ensuring that there was justice for the criminal. No one seemed to be considering the victims, and the struggle to achieve a fair balance continues today.

Ray's clear and committed objectives meant that he had little difficulty in persuading others to assist in any way they could. He achieved this through frequent talks to a wide variety of groups, and within a short period, to detectives and police officers in training.

One of the first requirements was to raise the profile of VSS and this was undertaken in several ways, most particularly through the newsletters, which widely distributed information and news as it became available. Among the most poignant and ironically, one of the most successful early events around this time, was Anne-Marie Mykyta's book, *It's a Long Road to Truro*, published in 1981 and referred to in chapter 2. Anne-Marie kept a diary during that terrible time upon which her book is based and, reading it now, the story is as painful and raw as if the events she described had occurred last week.

The book drew the public's attention to the aims of VSS and the services it provided, and should still be required reading for anyone involved in helping victims of crime.

Jenny

At last it was all over, the Magistrate having sentenced the offender to a period of detention. For Jenny, this was the culmination of more than a year of extreme stress and trauma.

Some 16 months earlier she had been seriously assaulted just as she was leaving her business premises in a suburban shopping centre. As usual Jenny had been working late in her stationery and card shop. There were often people popping in at the last moment on their way home from adjacent stores and she always tried to accommodate them. They had families to rush home to and only the cat was waiting for her.

Jenny turned out most of the lights after emptying the cash register and balancing the day's takings. As she moved to lock the front door it was forcefully pushed in, knocking her over as a man grabbed the money bag. Before she passed out, she recognised his face in the dim light – a regular customer.

A passer-by called the police after noticing that the door was half-open, and on investigation, found Jenny lying on the floor. She spent several days in hospital but was able to give the police a good description and the offender was picked up a few days later.

After some preliminary hearings, the matter was sent to the Magistrates Court 'Diversion Program', as it was deemed that the offender was intellectually impaired. To Jenny's horror, the offender was released on bail on two occasions but re-offended in both instances and was returned to custody.

Jenny and her Court Companion attended Court on many occasions over that period only to hear the matter adjourned again and again. She suffered a great deal of stress due to lack of communication and was sometimes not notified when a hearing date had been changed. A further difficulty arose when several different prosecutors were assigned to the case as a result of the drawn-out proceedings, each requiring a 'catch up' period, which meant repeating the evidence.

At long last the matter was resolved. The perpetrator was given a short custody sentence and a long period of supervision. Jenny has a strong character and a great deal of courage. She received some recompense from the Criminal Injuries Compensation scheme and has started a new business in another area. She is determined to succeed and not let the offender ruin her life.

Brochures

The first brochure, entitled *What happens next?* was produced in 1981 and designed to help victims of serious crime during the initial shock and confusion of being victimised. It was approved by the police department and then held over until it was felt that VSS had sufficient staff to meet an increasing demand from the northern suburbs. Ray admitted to some hesitation initially in case the ensuing requests for services exceeded the capacity of the volunteers to respond. The government finally launched it in December 1988.

In 1983 VSS was invited to submit an application for a grant to the Savings Bank of South Australia, to fund another publication. The application was successful and so *Are You a Victim of Crime?* was produced. The police agreed to hand this brochure to victims during early contact or at the crime scene. This became an important milestone in promoting good communi cation with the police department.

This was also the beginning of a significant catalogue of brochures available to the public and which cover a wide range of criminal and victim situations. What to do, who to contact, what is involved in going to court, how to claim compensation and much more. Over time so many leaflets and brochures were developed that they needed to be reorganised to reflect a 'corporate identity' and present a strong professional image. Thus, the layout and format were revamped in 1996–7 with the introduction of the new blue logo. The information is updated as necessary and now printed in several languages. For a full list of available brochures refer to the internet site www.victimsa.org or appendix 4.

The Police Victims of Crime Branch was launched in April 1999. Sergeant Michael O'Connell was appointed the Director of Victim Services attached to the Attorney-General's Department with the role of coordinating victim services in South Australia and works closely with VSS.

The constitution

The first constitution, drawn up by Richard Huxter was accepted in 1980. A new constitution was agreed in 1984 with only minor alterations: a Council of ten was recommended. A two-thirds majority at a general meeting could ratify changes to the constitution.

One of the changes was to require VSS to hold the annual general meeting between 1 March and 30 April each year. This separated it from the birthday parties, which continued to be held in September or October until the mid-1990s when both were again combined at an evening meeting.

In the early years the AGMs were held in Mead Hall adjacent to the Flinders Street Baptist Church on a Sunday at 12.30 pm, a convenient time after the morning service. Tea, coffee and soup were provided and members were encouraged to bring their own sandwich lunch, in effect an ecclesiastical picnic.

The Executive consisted of four: Ray Whitrod as Chairman, Barrie Hibbert, Vice Chairman and Geoff Pennell, Treasurer as before and the new

CEO (once a CEO was appointed). Their duties were primarily policy for-mulation and day-to-day administration. The recommendation for a new position of CEO was held back pending negotiations with the government for funding – the first step to employing professional staff.

Media

There continued to be articles in the media which highlight the services for victims and the push for changes to the law. In 1982 Anne-Marie Mykyta and Judy Barnes featured in a Channel 9 *60 Minutes* segment called 'Victim Help' and in 1992, there were two documentaries on the ABC. *Without Consent* was a feature on rape and domestic abuse, and an American film called *True Stories* concerned women who killed the men who had perpetrated such crimes. There have been others since.

In 1988 there was a period when it was felt that not enough people were aware of VSS services, so a community announcement was broadcast which rapidly increased calls for help and resulted in a rise in the number of people who visited the office. In 1989 *The Advertiser* invited Ray and a social worker to become part of the weekly panel called 'Family Forum' to which the public sent questions on a wide range of subjects, another small acknowledgment of the contribution VSS made to the community.

In December 1991 a fun event occurred when 100 teddy bears were donated to VSS to be taken to families with young children who had been traumatised. They were part of the 'Teddy Care' project undertaken by South Australia's 5000 Guides, for children less well off than they were. Some Guides made the bears, others contributed pocket money, all working to make some of these children happier than they had been for a while.

Some of the Teddy Bears

In recent years media articles have been written on topics such as child sexual abuse, improved facilities for vulnerable witnesses, crime statistics, the rising rate of crime and the fear of crime. The down side of harsher penalties and longer sentences without improved rehabilitation has been the subject of discussion on numerous occasions. The violence so often depicted in the media, especially in relation to advertising, films and books, has been high-lighted as encouraging crime.

Maintaining contact with the media has always been a two-way exchange at VSS, although at times it can seem unbalanced. Letters written to the press by senior VSS staff on subjects of importance aren't always published. Agreements to present a point of view through a series of articles can be displaced by other news and the pressures of time and space.

The August 1995 newsletter reported an interview with the then police reporter, Nick Papps, on the link between the media and the community. Nick agreed that the media could re-victimise those who have suffered from crime, but at the same time, he remarked, some victims felt a need to talk to the media to express their pain. Although some print and television media articles do not demonstrate the high standard of journalism required, it should be possible to be considerate to victims while being free from bias. Occasionally some reports are outstanding in their sensitivity and accuracy.

Every effort is made to work cooperatively with the media but VSS is not backward in disagreeing with or condemning errant elements. Especially targeted are those reporters who disregard principles of sensitive and accurate representation. In the annual report 2001–02 the Chief Executive Officer, Michael Dawson, writes:

> In the media we have always taken up a wide variety of issues – not least of which is continuing disgust about the media itself and the way it frequently treats victims ... Advocacy and community educa-tion through media is often a thankless task – but it is important to keep the faith and keep trying.

Mitchell Awards

In order to emphasise 'good' journalism, it was decided in the mid-1990s to reward excellent media reporting. The Governor of South Australia, Dame Roma Mitchell, an outstanding legal pioneer and member of the judiciary, agreed to give her name to the prizes and made the first presentations in June 1994.

Dame Roma Mitchell and Board Chairman Russell Jamison, 1994

The aim of the Mitchell Media Awards is to encourage the media to be accurate, objective and sensitive to victims' feelings and their need for privacy. They should also be willing to report on wider issues regarding victim rights and needs, and not simply focus on the sensational. Awards are presented in the categories of the Best Newspaper Journalist, Best Still Image Photographer, Best Television Item and Best Radio Station. They continue to be honoured every year.

Many volunteers have played an important role in assisting in the judging of the award recipients, including VSS member and former journalist Mike O'Reilly who provides expert input.

In 1999 after a number of years conducting 'in-house' media presentations ceremonies, VSS negotiated with the Institute of Justice Studies to join its much higher profile and well-recognised Justice Media Awards night. The Mitchell Media Award has gained further status and impact by becoming part of this event which the Governor of South Australia, executives of justice agencies and many media personalities attend.

Victim Awareness Week

Other media opportunities occurred during the first 'Victims' Awareness Week' in April 1993. The Police Band played in Rundle Mall and John Halsey, the Chairman of VSS at the time, introduced the Attorney-General, Chris Sumner, a representative of the SA Police Commissioner and Victim Contact Officers attached to the police force.

Many events took place during that special week, including eight new Court Companions in Port Augusta receiving their certificates and

The Advertiser printing a series of articles on victims of crime who had been assisted by Victim Support Service. Specially designed flags flew in Rundle Mall and King William Street, but the main focus was in Rundle Mall where volunteers staffed a booth, handed out brochures and answered questions.

A new promotional idea designed to raise community awareness of VSS was trialled at the 1995 Royal Adelaide Show. A display stand containing information about the organisation was erected with staff and volunteers in attendance.

A new style of 'Victim Awareness Week' was held from 1997–99 when VSS coordinated a larger event. The aim was to get other victim agencies to collaborate and become involved. Participants included the Homicide Victims' Support Group, the National Association for the Prevention of Child Abuse and Neglect, Compassionate Friends, Department of Public Prosecutions and Yarrow Place. Others who took part were the South Australia Police, Women's and Children's Hospital, Australasian Society of Victimology, the Crime Prevention Unit and the Gun Control Coalition of South Australia.

These events were extremely time-consuming for staff and volunteers, and as the media's interest in promoting victims' issues by supporting the community awareness week declined, attention was focused in other areas. Nevertheless, the Mitchell Media Awards continue and other events where VSS has a presence include Law Week and the South Australia 'Police Expo'.

Other opportunities for promotion became available in later years, including 'Volunteers Week', in which VSS took part. The Court Companion program won an award for excellence in 1996 and in 1999, the Public Speakers' Program received an award from the Premier for innovation.

Celebrating Victim Awareness Week

Reviews

Over the years the range of services provided by VSS and the needs of crime victims have been subject to review. The first took place in June 1980 when the State Government appointed an 'Inquiry into the Plight of Victims' and VSS was represented on the panel. The report was presented in March 1981 by the Attorney-General, Trevor Griffin, and contained 67 recommendations, presenting, as he later admitted, difficulties for total implementation.

Ray Whitrod described it as 'the first in the Western World to probe the specific needs of victims of crime'. Myk Mykyta was sceptical and commented that:

> It reads like a cheer for motherhood. The recommendations are full of laudable intentions but there is no assignment as to who or which department will carry them out. As long as that state of affairs exists everyone will congratulate themselves on being aware but nothing will be done to improve the conditions of the victims.

In fact, most of the recommendations were implemented by 1985 in spite of a change of government – which says a lot for the bi-partisan political support which VSS receives on behalf of victims. In October 1986 *The Advertiser* reported that approximately 600 victims of crime would be interviewed over the subsequent two years by three project officers from the Office of Crime Statistics in the Attorney-General's office, then Chris Sumner.

Ray Whitrod presented the first overview of VSS's progress after three years which is discussed elsewhere (refer chapter 9). The first full review of VSS itself was undertaken by an outsider, Ray Kidney, at the invitation of VSS and presented in January 1991. As the Executive Officer of OARS (Offenders' Aid and Rehabilitation Services of South Australia Incorporated) and a founder member of VSS, it could be expected that he would be knowledgeable, yet removed enough to be impartial.

However, a close study of his recommendations suggest a bias towards reducing costs by combining both organisations – VSS and OARS – in several areas, for example, through shared facilities, publications, publicity and support services. The implementation of these recommendations would have upset many VSS members who were, at that time, very wary of any association with criminal offenders, focusing fully on helping victims. Thus many suggestions were not followed through.

In other areas Ray Kidney was ahead of his time, such as recommending a program he had heard about when in America which facilitated offender–victim mediation and which was implemented with caution in South Australia several years later. Ray's other recommendations, such as extending group work, restructuring the Council and upgrading the newsletter were gradually adopted.

A major independent investigation of VSS with emphasis on the quality of management and client services was undertaken at the instigation of the Attorney-General, Trevor Griffin. The Review of Victims of Crime Service Inc., South Australia was presented in March 1996 and established the template for the future development of the organisation, including legislative change and support for the funding of regional services.

One of the main recommendations was for a regular strategic planning process to determine and establish aims and monitor progress. These have now been slotted into three-year time frames, which are subject to ongoing evaluation. Goals and priorities are developed as the result of various levels of consultation with the 'stakeholders'. In relation to VSS, they consist of the Board, the staff, the clients, the volunteers, the members and many other organisations with which VSS is associated – in fact, the community. The aims and outcomes are discussed in each year's annual report and the quarterly newsletters, a situation which leads to a very transparent style of management, while maintaining the necessary confidentiality.

Michael Dawson

Michael, the new CEO, was recruited in 1996 to develop planning and other strategies addressing future viability. These included human resource management, declining referral rates and loss of profile, occupational health and safety, relationships with government, connections with business, governance and commitment to volunteers.

Name change

At the half-yearly meeting on 12 August 1995 a name change was proposed for the organisation. It was believed the words, 'crime' and 'victim', had negative connotations. Moreover, there was a tendency for the public to be confused between VOCS and the Victims of Crime Branch of the SA Police. These and other changes to the constitution were accepted in May 1996. Thus VOCS became 'Victim Support Service Incorporated'. This occasion provided an opportunity for a new logo for which suggestions were invited (refer chapter 10).

Celebrations

In victory we deserve it. In defeat we need it. Champagne!

Sir Winston Churchill

Ray Whitrod loved a party, and almost any excuse would do to throw one. In the early years the annual general meetings and the VSS 'birthday parties' were held at the same time. This was an opportunity to bring people together to eat, drink (tea or coffee!) and feel proud and happy to be part of a hard-working group sharing their successes and difficulties.

The first birthday party was held at the Baptist Manse, Mead Hall on 25 October 1980 and 150 people attended. A video was shown of a documentary made by Sydney's Channel 10 called *Crime Victims* most of which was shot in Adelaide. The new logos commissioned by Bob Malin were on display for members to view and indicate their preference.

Barrie Hibbert's last birthday party before he and his wife went to work overseas was held on Sunday 12 October 1986. Prior to the festivities he conducted a church service in memory of victims. Ray described Barrie's address as 'crisp, challenging and inspirational'. Sir James Irwin and the Attorney-General, Chris Sumner read the Lessons.

Annual general meetings continued to be part-business and part-social occasions for many years. When they were first held separately, Ray admitted feeling nervous beforehand, worrying if anyone would come. He need not have worried, even business meetings brought out the loyal and long-time faithful. In 1990 he reported that the Attorney-General, Trevor Griffin and the Shadow Attorney-General, Chris Sumner attended and Sir Walter Crocker made his usual polished speech.

Sir Walter had been an active supporter of VSS behind the scenes from the early days. He was a former Lieutenant Governor of South Australia, an academic and a diplomat. He died in November 2002 aged 100 years.

Trevor Griffin was asked by Ray to look into his crystal ball and give an opinion on what VSS would look like in ten years' time. He admitted being rather stunned by the request but made a good stab at prophecy. Looking back, it is possible to see that he was not far wrong. Trevor predicted that counselling would continue to be of prime importance; that an increased range of brochures would be needed in languages other than English and that there should be no government control of VSS. It should stay an independent organisation 'firmly in control of a competent management committee providing service through volunteers guided by paid professionals'. Although the emphasis has slightly shifted to the professionals, this is basically the organisational model today.

He also advocated the establishment of a panel of speakers to address community groups, that VSS seek corporate sponsorship and that the organisation continue to strive for ready access to the media. All of these recommendations have been implemented over the intervening years.

'A Night to Remember', a large celebration dinner on 29 April 1993 was held at the Ramada Grand hotel at Glenelg.

Celebration dinner at the Ramada Hotel, 1993

It was a combined fund-raiser and recognition of VSS's founder and now Patron, Ray Whitrod and his wife Mavis. More than 150 people attended, representing all walks of life, including police, academics, banks, the corporate sector, the media, churches, VSS members and staff. The function provided an opportunity to thank Ray and his wife for their tremendous efforts over many years and to celebrate with his family, his recent Australia Day Honours Award of the Companion of the Order of Australia.

Another memorable milestone was the 20th birthday of VSS held on 22 September 1999 at the Halifax Street premises. There was a short formal annual general meeting which dealt with the business issues, followed by a *This is Your Life* occasion facilitated by lawyer and VSS member, Matthew Mitchell.

The evening was a fascinating and sometimes humorous journey through the organisation's first twenty years, which included perspectives from some of the very early members and video interviews with Ray and Harold Weir. There were presentations from Court Companions and staff, and the former Attorney-General, Chris Sumner, spoke about the changes in legislation over that period which had led to better outcomes for crime victims and survivors.

It was acknowledged that improvements were still needed but the evening gave the audience an appreciation of how much can be achieved both by individuals and groups of like-minded people with common goals.

So how were those changes accomplished?

5. Location, location

Life in our office is very much like life in the armed forces - there are long periods of boredom and frustration, interspersed with feverish activity.

Ray Whitrod

As children growing up, our memories of good and bad experiences tend to be linked with smells, sounds, the cold of winter or the heat of summer. Our school years are often a mixture of fun, facts, pain and friendship. These links continue into adulthood where we experience many triggers which take us back to people and places we have not seen for years and which are the source of so many memories.

That is how it is with VSS, which started operations in borrowed space in October 1979, thanks to the Reverend Barrie Hibbert. Mead Hall was the Manse of Flinders Street Baptist Church at 65 Flinders Street in the Adelaide city centre, and at least two meetings were held there.

Not wishing to take advantage of the church's hospitality, Ray Whitrod approached the Public Buildings Department for unoccupied space. Much to his delight, two weeks later VSS had the use of four fully repaired and freshly painted rooms at 61 Flinders Street (Charlick House), just a few doors away.

Max Dawson, a friend of Ray's from Scouting days, recalls being roped in to do the painting, while Ray 'was running hither and thither scrounging carpets, tables, chairs, you name it, anything he could get his hands on, to furnish the place'. Many people and organisations gave a variety of items and money towards making the offices comfortable, and Mabarrack Bros,

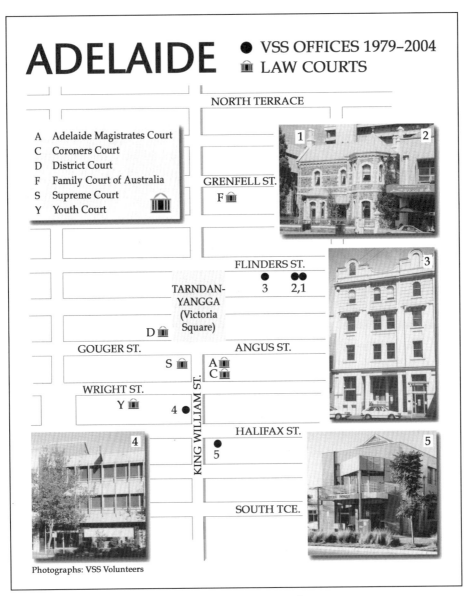

ADELAIDE

● VSS OFFICES 1979–2004
🏛 LAW COURTS

NORTH TERRACE

A   Adelaide Magistrates Court
C   Coroners Court
D   District Court
F   Family Court of Australia
S   Supreme Court
Y   Youth Court

GRENFELL ST.

F 🏛

FLINDERS ST.

TARNDAN-
YANGGA
(Victoria
Square)

D 🏛

● ●●
3   2,1

GOUGER ST.

ANGUS ST.

S 🏛   A 🏛
C 🏛

WRIGHT ST.

Y 🏛   4 ●

KING WILLIAM ST.

HALIFAX ST.

● 5

SOUTH TCE.

Photographs: VSS Volunteers

Map of locations (VSS) and nearby courts

a family furniture business, generously donated a large, round coffee table, which is still in use in the current premises.

The office was officially open from 10.30 am to 3 pm, Mondays to Fridays. For many years Ray Whitrod's home phone was the after-hours contact number. The comfort of their new quarters was short-lived – from November 1979 until May 1980 in fact. It wasn't long before Ray received a call to say that Charlick House was to be sold and VSS would have to move again.

Approaches were made to the Minister for Public Buildings, Dean Brown, requesting permission for occupancy of unused government office space. Ray was grateful for the speedy response but the next move was to three smaller offices in Liverpool Building, 49–51 Flinders Street, where meetings commenced in May 1980 and which the Public Buildings Department made some attempt to decorate. Here they stayed in increasing discomfort for the next eleven-and-a-half years.

A fridge donated by Mr and Mrs Andrew Ridland and very much appreciated, provided some drama when it was hoisted up to the second floor through a window, which had to be dismantled for the exercise. More on that later.

The accommodation was cramped but Ray referred to it as 'The Ritz' in honour of the wonderful lunches Ritsie Pennell supplied for Tuesday meetings. Ritsie and her husband Geoff attended the office two or three days a week, and Geoff eventually became Treasurer. They undertook whatever job was required, manning the phone and folding and sending the newsletters.

In spite of Ray's flattering title for the office, the reality of 'The Ritz' was closer to John Oliphant's description (one of the early social workers and later senior social worker):

> The Flinders Street premise was an extraordinary building; working there was an experience in itself. It was very run down, my impression was that it was a building waiting to be demolished; no one was going to spend any money on it. When you worked there you really had to dress for the weather because in winter it was freezing and in summer one fried in the heat. After I had been there a few days, I remember noticing how cold one of the corridors was, every time I walked down, it was freezing. I stopped one day and realised there was no glass in one of the windows. Obviously the window had been broken over time, and rather than fixing it, they just removed all the glass so that you couldn't actually see it was broken. No wonder it was cold!

On another occasion John explored the wooden fire escape.

We went down this wooden staircase and it took you to a doorway out of the building with a metal ladder going down, which stopped about thirty feet above the ground. It wouldn't have passed the fire safety test!

Likewise, the ancient, rickety lift was so nerve-wracking that clients were advised to walk up the stairs. It was quicker and less traumatising! Working in the Liverpool Building clearly required a sense of humour or at least a certain toughness.

Ray wrote the 'Just Another Newsletter' story in August 1988 following a sojourn in hospital that year. The following is a slightly abbreviated version:

Peter and Joyce Presnail (the only members who could work the duplicating machine) started work at noon one day to get out the June newsletter. Other staff left at 5 pm but Peter and Joyce kept going to finish the job by 7.30 pm. They turned off the lights, pushed the release mechanism in the deadlock before pulling the door closed behind them. The lock slide jammed and the door would not close.

With no key and a faulty deadlock they decided to phone Des House (the Administration Officer) for help. A new Commander phone system had recently been installed and Peter couldn't make it work as it had been switched to the answering machine. He and Joyce pulled out a few plugs trying to isolate the answering machine but to no avail, so they gave up and Peter went off to find a public phone.

Fifteen minutes later Des arrived to find Peter outside the building looking a bit the worse for wear. 'We have another problem', he said. 'When I went to find a phone someone else left the building and locked the main entrance behind them'.

'No problem', said Des, 'We'll phone Joyce and ask her to come down and unlock the front door'. No answer – the phone was dead as a result of the plugs being pulled out.

'No problem', said Des again, 'We'll phone someone else in the building'. They called every business they could think of, but with no response. Now there was a crisis and they headed to the back lane behind the building. The time was 8.30 pm.

They could see the office lights were on, two floors up but

couldn't make contact. Peter called 'Joyce! Joyce!', his voice echoing down the empty back lanes. Des threw handfuls of large bark chips before falling over in a fit of laughter.

'Joyce! Joyce!' called Peter and an echoing voice nearby replied 'Hello! Hello!' A few passers-by took off at a great rate at the sight of vandals yelling and throwing objects at the building.

No luck. After more thought, a brilliant plan! Climb up the fire escape, open the fire escape door on the second floor and all would be solved. The only problem was that the bottom of the fire escape was out of reach. Not to be beaten, Des suggested he run round to the front of the building, drive his car to the back, park it under the ladder, climb onto the car roof and grab the bottom rung of the fire escape. No worries!

So Des ran to the front of the building and surprise, surprise! There stood a worried and cold Joyce anxiously waiting for Peter. So they all went upstairs, fixed the lock, replaced the plugs, had a good laugh and left just after 9 pm.

In 1988 VSS was informed that a move from the crowded and inadequate offices in Liverpool Building would be necessary as it was to be sold. This move finally occurred in December 1991 when VSS took possession of more spacious accommodation at 339 King William Street, not far away, and which was formally opened by the Attorney-General, Chris Sumner in July 1992.

Again the offices were on the second floor but there was no way the long-serving fridge would be left behind. There was a general reluctance to dismantle a window yet again, so Andrew Paterson, then Executive Director had the bright idea of asking the Fire Brigade if they were due for an exercise. No problem! Four eager beavers arrived with a rescue crane and easily removed the refrigerator through the fire escape door and brought it down to earth. From there the removalists were able to take it to the new offices using the safer lift in the new building. Full marks for the Fire Brigade's community service!

Staff and volunteers have many never-to-be-forgotten memories of their times with the VSS – depending on where the office was located at the time. One thing is certain, it was never boring and it still isn't.

Six years later, in December 1997, VSS was on the move again due to increasing workloads, the need for more security and better facilities. The

Lifting the fridge

next home for VSS was located just around the corner at 11 Halifax Street and fortunately in ground-floor, shop-front premises. They are bright, light, relatively spacious, accessible and welcoming to visitors and crime victims. VSS is still housed in these offices.

One of VSS's greatest supporters is Kate Lennon, Chief Executive of the Justice and Attorney-General's departments. She once reflected that victims of crime deserve pleasant and professional accommodation. The present offices are by far the most comfortable and convenient premises to date, but at the time of writing, it is envisaged that eventually more space will be needed, as activities have expanded exponentially and referrals increase every year. The number of meetings held each week have, of necessity, increased and once again offices are being shared. Another move may be necessary at a future date, but leaving Halifax Street will be a mixed blessing, since so many good memories reside there.

6. The Court Companions

Life is mainly froth and bubble
Two things stand like stone,
Kindness in another's trouble
Courage in your own.

Constable Adam Lindsay Gordon

Can you imagine attending court as a witness because you are somehow involved in a crime, even second or third hand? Could you cope with the gut-wrenching fear and anxiety, which builds up prior to the experience? This is on top of any grief or injury which you may have already suffered.

The after-effects engendered by a home invasion or having your car stolen and trashed are unpleasant, almost intolerable experiences in themselves. These and other crimes are a personal affront, and having to attend court compounds the physical and psychological stress.

Many people naturally want to have a family member or friend with them for support during this time, but this is not always possible. A good solution is to have a Court Companion by your side, because facing the criminal justice system, the police, courts and media is sometimes so traumatic that it is described as 'secondary victimisation'.

A Court Companion is 'A trained volunteer who provides support, friendship, comfort and information to a victim of crime at the time they are required to appear in court'. The concept of Court Companions evolved just as the Truro Murders Trial got under way as the need to support victims became apparent. The recognition of this need became one of the primary reasons for the formation of Victim Support Service. Ray Whitrod wrote:

Victims as witnesses complained that they weren't sure where to go, or what was required of them, they didn't understand the procedure. They felt lonely and sometimes frightened, and occasionally needed a friendly shoulder to cry upon when they were forced to relive frightening experiences, especially when their attacker was again present.

Other problems reported by victims include 'feeling guilty' when giving evidence, as if they themselves are on trial (witnesses have no legal representation). They may also have difficulties with the processes of Victim Impact Statements, criminal injuries compensation and sentencing. On occasions the victims themselves may be blamed by the community, which aggravates their distress. Family members of victims are left out of the plea-bargaining and parole assessments. Many of these issues have been addressed in the new *Victims of Crime Act* (refer chapter 14).

The very first Court Companions in South Australia were Mavis and Ray Whitrod, and for several years, theirs was the after-hours phone number for victims in crisis, later shared by others. The first organised group arose out of a talk Ray gave in 1981 to the Dental Wives Group led by Babs Horsnell. The Dental Wives took up the challenge and monthly meetings were soon held in Althea Walker's home and she became the coordinator and Ray's contact person. When she had to resign after several years for personal reasons, the job was taken over by Joan Young.

Senior police and judiciary supported the concept of Court Companions and offered to assist with the training.

It took some time to produce brochures and educate detectives and others who had had first contact with victims of crime, but once the idea caught on, there were times when the Court Companions could not meet the demand. In 1987 the South Australian Police Commissioner, David Hunt, established a Victim Branch in the Police Department, the first in Australia, the staff of which work closely with a local victim service.

The early emphasis was on long-term friendship and occasionally Court Companions visited victims in their homes. 'We do claim to offer long-term friendship, rather than the hit-run contact provided by some', Ray wrote in the newsletter of October 1986. Now the policy is that only professional VSS staff undertake home visits.

At that time it was not unusual to have two Court Companions to accompany a victim to court. This enabled them to give each other a break or to look after other members of the family. It has also been reported that two Court Companions stayed with the mother of one victim each day the court was in session for nearly six months.

The Farmer

Bill the farmer is in his 50s, hard-working and single, having always lived with his parents, looking after them until they died. Now he lives alone, devoted to his animals and his church. His pleasures are keeping his sheep and dogs healthy and meeting fellow parishioners on Sundays.

One day, on returning from food shopping he discovers his utility has gone and with it Oscar, his favourite sheep – they all have names. He reports his loss to the police and the next day they phone and say his ute has been found with the tray covered in blood. Three teenage boys aged 13, 15 and 16 years are later apprehended, charged with stealing and told to report to a Family Conference, an alternative option for under-18s who confess to a charge which is at the lower end of severity.

An adult male with whom they live, accompanies all the boys; none of them have parents present. Their dark expressions range from sullenness to defiance. Representatives from the RSPCA are also at the conference, as one of the charges is 'cruelty to animals'.

Bill attends with a Court Companion for support. He is very nervous but even more angry and upset. When it's his turn to speak, stammering, he asks the boys why they had tortured his beloved Oscar and then barbequed him. They just glare. He went on to tell them how much his animals mean to him; that they barely earn him a living but are precious companions along with his dogs.

Suddenly everyone in the room is aware of the silent tears running down Bill's cheeks. The boys drop their heads and with defensive whines, mutter about sleeping rough and being hungry.

After a great deal of discussion the boys receive a variety of negotiated penalties. They range from letters of apology, compensation from the older two and community service, which includes caring for abandoned dogs in an animal shelter. It is suggested that one option could be working for the farmer but he said he didn't feel comfortable with that idea.

Outside the court a calmer Bill turns to the Court Companion and says, 'Well, I'm glad I came and thanks for coming with me. I feel rather sorry for them, really'.

It is important for a Court Companion to be impartial. Ray describes an occasion when, as a Court Companion, he accompanied the victim's wife to court. The wife of the accused who was an acquaintance, challenged him with 'Surely you don't believe *her* story?' Ray pointed out that, since VSS Court Companions do not have access to all the facts, it is important not to make judgements which rely on information given by the referring police officer or other community workers when they refer victims. (Victims of crime can self-refer to VSS if they wish.)

This policy was supported by an article in *The Advertiser* (8 June 1984) which claimed that liability, that is the risk of being sued for wrongful advice, can exist if advice is given voluntarily and orally. This was seen as a warning to Court Companions to be friends rather than advisers. It should be noted that Court Companions are not provided for defendants or their families, the emphasis being that VSS is working for victims.

Court Companion training

Small people, casual remarks and little things, very often shape our lives more powerfully, than the deliberate, solemn advice of great people at critical moments.

Sir Winston Churchill

Court Companions are volunteers, male and female, who have applied in writing with two references. There is an initial interview and a police check. Once accepted into the training course, which usually lasts three days, the program consists of presentations on the impact of victimisation, legal processes, court procedures, the role of the Court Companion and communication skills.

At the end of the course another interview is conducted and selection is confirmed. There is usually one training program a year. New graduates of the Court Companion course may attend court with a 'buddy' at first, until they have gained confidence and experience. All VSS volunteers, including Court Companions, may be reimbursed for out-of-pocket expenses such as transport, parking etc.

The qualities needed to be a Court Companion include compassion, commitment, confidence, and an outgoing but calm manner. These skills are especially required when supporting a stressed client who has been called as a witness. Maintaining confidentially is an obligation and the ability to work as part of a team is essential.

Group of Court Companions

Court Companions are familiar with the layout of courts and aware of court procedures and processes. They may not express their own views on a case nor permit discussion of it while the person they are accompanying is waiting to give evidence or is due back in court. In other words, it is imperative to avoid influencing a witness in any way. At times this can be very difficult during the process of providing emotional support.

On one occasion a court officer believed that he discerned a signal passing between a witness and the Court Companion during a case. The Court Companion was called to speak to the judge. The suspicion proved groundless but the incident highlighted the ease with which a trial could be aborted on a seemingly innocent, but important technicality.

Court Companions may arrange to meet their clients before the hearing over a cup of coffee or talk to them by phone. They will access safe waiting areas and can be present in court with clients and liaise with court staff on their behalf. Court Companions may also accompany crime victims to make a statement to police if needed.

A Court Companion may not transport a client in their own car, reveal their surname or phone numbers or supply any medication, not even something as straightforward as paracetamol. Court Companions will not provide a baby-sitting service or give legal advice. They are not counsellors or bodyguards. Court staff, known as Sheriff's Officers are available as back up in an emergency.

Allowing for the legal constraints, a Court Companion can make a court visit an enlightening and less stressful event. Their training, experience and calm approach, while supplying emotional and practical support, can make the difference between feeling very scared and very safe.

Monthly meetings are held at VSS for all Court Companions able to attend to discuss relevant issues and share information. Additional training is available on specific subjects from time to time, and speakers from other agencies are invited to talk about their expertise in relevant areas. Site visits to prisons and courts can be arranged if requested, although this does not occur on a regular basis.

Barbara Agacy

One of the longest serving Court Companions is Barbara who arrived in Adelaide from India with her husband and two daughters in 1969. Sadly her husband died 15 months later. After working for a few years, in 1982 Barbara met Ray Whitrod and joined VSS, training as a Court Companion. At the time of writing she is still assisting people who need to attend court.

Joan Cornish

Joan Cornish

Another outstanding and long-serving volunteer was Joan Cornish who initially contacted VSS as a victim in 1987. She later contributed to the setting up of the Ongoing Women's Group, becoming a dedicated helper and supporter of others.

In 1991 Joan joined the Court Companion program and her relaxed and reassuring manner helped many victims through the stress of the court process. The following year she was elected to the Board of Management where she served for seven years, always ensuring the victim's point of view was considered during discussions.

In 1997 she undertook the specific training to become a member of the Public Speakers' Group where her natural talent in this area became apparent. With her easy ability to talk to anyone, a sincere concern for the welfare of others and her sense of humour, she was great to have around. In the VSS office she would pick up any job which required attention and quietly get on with it. Her unexpected death in July 1999 came as a great shock and loss to her family and the many friends who had come to consider her indispensable.

Victim Support Service is fortunate in continuing to attract such special people to provide volunteer court services and in being able to work closely with associated organisations.

7. Connections – anyone else out there?

A rising tide lifts all boats.

J. F. Kennedy

It's always exciting to be the first to develop something new, but the foremost feelings of the victims facing up to the Truro Murder Trial in 1979 were a combination of grief, anxiety and relief, relief that at last, thanks to 'VOCS', they were not alone and that a group of people had banded together to provide support, care and understanding.

South Australia's Victim Support Service was one of the earliest agencies of its type in the developed world, the first in Australia and it is still considered one of the best. It is now the largest non-government victims' service in Australia. In the early 1980s there was a flurry of interest following the establishment of VSS, and in the following year, a local branch was inaugurated in Tasmania, using South Australia's letterhead, and soon had a membership of three hundred.

Ray wasted no time in creating links with other organisations and drawing attention to achievements in other areas to highlight the need at home. At a public talk only nine months after the establishment of VOCS, he referred to the Victim Compensation Scheme which commenced in 1963, as worth investigating.

Ray also mentioned that, in 1975, Gerald Ford, then President of the United States had commented that, for too long, the rights of the criminal had taken precedence over the rights of the victims and it was time this trend was reversed. This led to an increase in compensation and an expansion of services to victims in America. In 1979 the British Government also provided an annual grant for local victims' support groups.

Nearer home, in November 1979, a national opinion poll was conducted to determine whether the community believed that police should have stronger powers in maintaining law and order. The highest positive figure of 78 per cent came from Adelaide, which probably reflected the detailed reporting of the Truro Murder Trial at the time.

Thanks to the energy of Ray Whitrod and his team, people in other states were motivated to develop similar organisations and experienced similar ebbs and flows in raising membership and finance. Melbourne Police were very keen to start VOCAL (Victims of Crime Assistance League) and there were enquiries from West Australia, Darwin and Maroubra in New South Wales.

Something else was needed. It turned out to be sheer hard work.

Early in 1982 Ray attended a workshop at Sydney University with the Australian Bureau of Statistics to discuss the collection of crime figures. He was able to meet representatives from the VOCAL and Maroubra groups, but in Western Australia, people were having difficulty getting similar groups up and running. A new victim organisation started in Perth in 1983 and there were consistent efforts between the states to combine the organisations, culminating in August 1988 in the establishment of The Australasian Society of Victimology which was based in Adelaide.

Its objectives were to promote research, focus attention on the needs of victims and encourage cooperation and exchange of information about victims. It hosted the International Victimology Symposium in 1984, has contributed funds to several victims' conferences and still exists today. Chris Sumner, Michael O'Connell (Victims of Crime Coordinator) and Michael Dawson, CEO of VSS are still active on the executive committee.

In 1989, at a police commissioners conference, it was pointed out that ten years earlier all states had attempted to follow South Australia's lead in establishing victim support groups. At first all went well and Ray was appointed as national spokesman. Eventually however, all failed except those in Melbourne and Adelaide. Nevertheless, persistence gradually paid off and all states now have victim support organisations. Commissioner David Hunt from South Australia persuaded the conference to release a statement calling on all state governments to adopt the United Nations

Declaration of Human Rights, which so far had occurred only in South Australia.

In England the British Association of Support Schemes held its second annual meeting in London in 1982 and reported that 114 towns had established branches. In 1990 the renamed National Association of Victim Support Services (NAVSS) received £11 million to develop a nationwide network of groups – all from a single group started by two probation officers. Each day the police give the local support group a list of victims' names and addresses for members to visit. This was usually a volunteer supervised by paid staff.

The World Society of Victimology was established in Germany in 1982 and Ray became a member of the small international executive. In the beginning this was a combined Australian, British and American organisation.

On 14 August 1985 Ray visited Yugoslavia to attend the 5th International Symposium on Victimology. From there he travelled to Milan as the only victim representative in the Australian delegation to the 7th United Nations Congress on the Prevention of Crime and the Treatment of Offenders.

After one of his trips Ray wrote:

> If you have never travelled with Yugoslav Air then you have missed one of life's great adventures. Mind you, you only need to do it once. It's a casual affair with all the give and take of a large family. If you were RAAF trained like me to be on time over the target within thirty seconds, then you will need to do more than just adjust your seat belt on take off.

In 1986 Ray made his third visit to Yugoslavia in two years and describes giving a talk on victimology to post-graduate students at a university. The other lecturers were lawyers and academics and the process was very formal. Ray's lecture was the fifth on the program and he felt by then the audience was getting tired. He decided to liven up the proceedings with overheads, handouts and a steady supply of Minties. Although English was not their first language he said they appreciated the motto 'It's at moments like these!'

Also held in 1985 was the convention of the American National Organisation for Victims Assistance (NOVA). After this event Ray noted that: 'They lead the world in victim assistance practices. Our little, struggling groups in Australia can learn much from them'. In September 1993 Andrew Paterson, then Executive Director of VSS was invited by NOVA to the United States to present a seminar at a conference.

For his part, Ray visited Japan during the early 1980s and described the dearth of victim services at the time. The 8th International Symposium on Victimology held in Adelaide in 1994 featured several Japanese speakers who described the commencement of victim services in that country two years earlier, albeit handicapped by a culture of shame at becoming a victim.

Professor Masao Okumura from Seiwa University gave a paper based on a survey of victims who had been asked what services were required after a crime in terms of follow-up assistance and further information. The responses included rescue from current danger, immediate support and comfort, information and help from the police. The concepts of long-term support for victims and the value of Court Companions seemed to be missing at that time in Japan. At least a beginning was being made compared with many countries where victims' rights are still virtually non-existent.

It can be seen from the examples cited above that reports of the activities of the young VSS organisation were spreading around the world, and more than twenty years on, people working in victim support in other countries are still aware of the early pioneering work emanating from Adelaide.

Every three years Michael Dawson represents South Australia at international victimology symposia with the assistance of funding from the Attorney-General's Department. In this way the VSS model of victim care has been taken to Holland, Canada and South Africa.

In 1990 representatives from five states – known as the Canberra Consultation – discussed setting up a national body to promote policies and programs which would enable the combined groups to speak with one voice, especially when approaching governments. In 1992 the established victim support services from the states involved met to inaugurate the Australasian Victims of Crime Association for the purpose of promoting the rights of victims and their families during involvement with the criminal justice system.

Double Take

It was a clear, chilly autumn day, when David, a pleasant, quiet man in his thirties, working in a large northern town, went for his usual stroll through the park during the lunch break. Without warning he was struck from behind and fell to the ground. Later he was told that a studded leather belt, left beside him, had been used to inflict extensive injuries to the back of his head.

He lay in a foggy haze, unable to move but aware that people were walking past, slowing down but moving away from him. He tried to speak but couldn't. Eventually a man did stop and used his mobile phone to call for police and ambulance. David spent the next two days in hospital but was assured that, although his injuries were less serious than at first appeared, he should spend a week at home, resting, before returning to work.

The offender, an elderly vagrant, who was known to the police, was later identified, charged, held on remand and booked to appear in the local magistrate's court.

Following the assault, David experienced many reactions, including loss of confidence, nightmares and extreme fatigue. The unnerving thought of fronting up to court in this state, encouraged him to seek help from Victim Support Service. He received counselling and was assured that his physical and psychological symptoms were normal, but that he might like to be accompanied to court by a Court Companion. He accepted with relief as his wife was pregnant and unavailable.

By the time the date for the magistrate's hearing arrived, David was feeling better. With the support of his Court Companion, whom he had already met, the experience of attending court did not worry him and seeing the frail, mentally disturbed defendant aroused more pity than anger.

After responding to questions and telling his story, David said it was his wish that the offender, who appeared to be very disadvantaged, be given appropriate help. He hoped that with assistance the man could lead a more normal life in the future.

The magistrate commended David for his attitude and made the necessary orders for accommodation and ongoing supervision.

The sad irony of such a generous gesture was that while David was lying helpless on the pavement, someone stole his expensive sunglasses.

The name of the organisation was changed to Victim Support Australasia in 1997 and its membership broadened to include any victim agency. Once a year, all the members from Australia and New Zealand meet to address national issues and develop strategies. Through Andrew Paterson and Michael Dawson with support from the Board, VSS has always displayed a strong commitment to this body and contributed to across-border developments.

Local connections

The 1997–98 Victim Support Service annual report included detailed contributions from other agencies with whom they work. The Victim Contact Officers with the South Australia Police reported that the good partnership between them resulted in better outcomes for victims and that they enjoyed the interaction. A strong relationship also exists with the Witness Assistance Service whose staff assists in training Court Companions, and with the Department of Public Prosecutions as a whole.

The Cavan Training Centre, which is managed by the Family and Youth Services Division (Department of Human Services), began running Victim Awareness Programs in 1993. The program's main aim is to raise the level of awareness in young offenders of the effect that crime has on the victim and the community as a whole. Staff from VSS regularly participate in this program.

The first awareness program for adults commenced at Mobilong Prison in 1997. It was designed and delivered by Andrew Paterson, then General Manager of the prison and Michael Dawson, currently VSS CEO. The content has been changed by the Department for Correctional Services in recent years, but VSS still contributes to sessions run with offenders in Adelaide and through its regional services.

Neighbourhood Watch often requests that one of the Public Speakers' Panel address a meeting about the services available for victims. Yarrow Place – Rape and Sexual Assault Service is another agency with close ties to VSS. This organisation collaborates with VSS in many ways, including having a VSS staff member on their Board of Management as do the Management Committees of the Mental Impairment and Drug Courts.

Other cooperative arrangements and connections have been established. For example, Michael Dawson, has been elected to the South Australian Council of Social Services (SACOSS) Board and Policy Council where crime victim issues are now reflected in submissions to Cabinet and government ministers. Michael was also invited to be an inaugural member of the Centre for Restorative Justice to promote better processes for victims. A formal memorandum of understanding has been developed with the South Australia Police, providing a very close working relationship in many areas. The CEO was also invited to be a member of the Council of Offenders Aid and Rehabilitation Service (OARS), reflecting a new level of understanding between VSS and offenders groups. Michael Dawson provides input to the

Australian Crime Prevention Council in relation to crime victims and the links between prevention and reducing the impact of victimisation.

In addition to the more formal organisations in Australia and around the world there are many private, independent groups of people who have combined to address the effects of specific crimes. Some disband when the aims are met, others are ongoing.

For example, in 1981 in the United States, a group of women formed MADD – Mothers Against Drink Driving – after a girl walking her bike at the side of the road was killed. The driver was drunk and had been released on bail two days earlier for a similar offence. Parents began campaigning on this issue, and by 1983 there were 85 branches in 29 states focusing on teenage drunk drivers. Also in America, POMC – Parents Of Murdered Children – was inaugurated in 1978 by Robert and Charlotte Hullinger whose teenage daughter had been killed. By 1982 there was a national network of 20 chapters which met monthly and published a quarterly journal entitled *Survivors*.

Similar groups have been established both in South Australia and interstate where they are usually under the auspices of VSS (refer chapter 12). By working together with a variety of organisations concerned with crime, its prevention and the rehabilitation of offenders, VSS promotes rapport and better understanding.

For victims of crime, understanding is so important and not always readily available. As David Pemberthy wrote in the newsletter of November 1994, 'The media loves crime because people hate (or love to hate) reading about crime'. For organisations like VSS, working with victims and for legislative reforms in victimology, this is both a problem and a solution.

8. Keeping tabs – money and members

Never ask of money spent
Where the spender thinks it went.
Nobody was ever meant
To remember or invent
What he did with every cent.

'The Hardship of Accounting' Robert Frost (1936)

The twin issues of membership and finance were always inextricably woven in the early years, pressure on one affecting the other, but for the sake of clarity they will be addressed separately.

Membership

A member a day helps keep the criminal away.

Jingle used in early membership drives

The often desperate push for members reflected the need for subscriptions and donations, however modest, both to retain independence and to increase the credibility of the organisation. In the opinion of governments and the community, growing public support indicated that VSS was meeting the expanding demand for services.

Ray Whitrod and others gave a huge number of talks to a variety of church and special interest clubs, which included the Retired Union Members' Association, retired business and professional men's organisations, Probus, Rotary and church groups. His aims were to inform listeners about the plight of victims, encourage membership and keep a lookout for possible assistants for VSS.

On one occasion he wrote that he needed 500 heads mulling over problem-solving, exercising their grey cells and that having reached the magic age of 80 would not be accepted as an excuse. Ray was driven by the constant need for new members. When discussing recruitment, he always asked *How? Why?* and *Why Not?* No problems were insurmountable – everything could be solved by persistence and determination, and he had plenty of both. In the 1980s Ray estimated that he had spent at least 2000 hours (unpaid, of course) a year working for VSS, which included one hour for each new, recruited member. The actual total was probably much more. He wasn't complaining, simply pointing out that commitment was necessary and time-consuming, and the greater the numbers who assisted, the better the outcome.

At the December meeting in 1980 he set a goal of seven new people to be recruited by each member with a target of 3000 for the coming year. This was clearly an onerous and impossible task but Ray never stopped trying to attract new blood and talent to the organisation. He was fond of quoting David Everett's (1770–1813) line 'Tall oaks from little acorns grow'.

> *In Germany in 1977 a journalist had produced a national television series on victims of crime. It resulted in the formation in June of that year, of a victim support group called The White Ring which was supervised in each province by the local Police Commissioner. In 1980 Ray reported in the newsletter that the organisation had 10,000 members, each contributing the equivalent of $1.50 each week from their pay packet. The prize for the person recruiting the most new members was a cruise on the Rhine. It was clear that 'Popeye' on the Torrens would not quite measure up!*

Looking back it seems that the goals could be interpreted as unrealistic, but working on the premise it is better to be ambitious and aim high, the attitude was always positive. Ray was not *always* fortunate in enrolling new members. He once reported:

Churchmen's dinner; had a nice meal and nothing else. Port Lincoln, an enthusiastic audience, a raffle netted $70 but no new members. A gathering of 200 churchmen at Brighton and only 11 new members.

Ray fretted and fumed about the need for more support but actually the membership increased gradually every year thanks to the tremendous effort he and others put in. Pushing it up to 2000 was a great achievement even although at the time it didn't appear to be enough or the right people!

A well-known member in 1984 was Dr John Cornwall, then South Australia's Minister of Health. It never hurts to name-drop when trying to raise funds for a good cause! In 1985 a goal of 5000 members was mooted but over the years the number has usually vacillated between one and two thousand. Ray commented that:

> Membership in the metropolitan area tends to come from retired folk, Church fellowships, service clubs, so that the younger generation are under-represented. Support is slightly more widespread in the country, and numerically stronger in proportion to population.

In 1988 Ray again urged increased membership, which at that time, counting 'marrieds' was around 1800. His argument was that more members represented a stronger lobby group, although this emphasis discounts the effectiveness of his professional approach and extensive contacts, which were always employed when making representations. Ray also noted that VSS had an unusually low turnover rate when compared with similar establishments, and when someone did leave the direction was usually 'geographical or heavenly'.

Ray's concern to remain apolitical in seeking government support was evident, given his awareness that the broad recruitment strategies ensured a wide range of opinions. Ray noted that while it was valid to air a range of opinions at some stage, he felt that since emotions can become heated on some issues, it was better to concentrate on areas where there was wide-spread support.

> Within the membership of VOCS there is a wide spectrum of opinion, political and social. We are united in seeking a better deal for crime victims and if we confine ourselves to that aim we should not dis-integrate into splinter groups, argue endlessly about such difficult matters as the possible reintroduction of capital punishment.

In 1982, during a rural downturn, Ray's attention was drawn to the fact that many members might find even the minimal membership fee more than they could afford. Ray emphasised that commitment was more impor-tant than money. He wrote:

> We are a family, not an organisation and at VOCS office we look upon all of you as good friends.

Early in 1990 the newsletter reported that Mr Elliott Starrick who lived in the small Adelaide Hills town of Springton had single-handedly enrolled 200 new members in just over two months.

Elliott Starrick

Every member was encouraged to visit the office when they had time and, in the interests of open administration, a log of events, including recent decisions, was maintained there for inspection.

As society has changed and volunteerism declined to an all-time low in the developed world, VSS membership has also declined. Early members, many from church organisations are deceased, have become ill or are unable to follow victims' issues. The Board recognises this decline in individual membership and has agreed that membership of a complex service delivery organisation is more likely to occur through other organisations and their personnel. VSS is now too large to rely heavily on individual member's fees and donations. It needs to access larger grants.

While membership reflects trends in modern society, the volunteer commitment is as strong as ever and numbers keep growing. The volunteers and members of VSS are those who are particularly interested in victims' issues, a situation which enables the organisation to speak and advocate confidently on behalf of a still large group of people. This aspect of membership is important.

Finance

Why is there so much month left at the end of the money?

Anon

At the inaugural meeting of VSS one of the aims was to be 'self-sufficient'. That translated to being financially independent of the government. Apart from members' fees the organisation depended on donations, gifts and government generosity in permitting occupation of empty office space in order to continue. Many letters of appreciation on file originally included donations and they often followed a meeting which Ray had reported as disappointing!

One of the first administrative actions was to approach the Australian Taxation Office to authorise tax-deductible donations, which was eventually approved. Because of the number of times that membership drives and money are mentioned in newsletters, one can assume that both were a continuing source of worry.

In the 1982 'third year report' Ray writes:

> The smallness of our expenditure is largely due to the generosity of our volunteers in not seeking reimbursement of any costs, so this has enabled us to achieve another of our targets – that of self-sufficiency – that we originally agreed upon.

Man's best friend

John, a man in his thirties had known the Harris family for ten years, through membership of their local Church where he had held a position of trust and responsibility as finance manager. Jean and Tom Harris had confidence in him and when they retired in their early sixties and decided to visit Tasmania they asked John to look after their house and agreed he could move in while they were away for the six weeks.

They were called back early by their married daughter who felt that John was behaving suspiciously whenever she visited her parents' house. When they got back they found that their television, VCR and several valuable pieces of jewellery were missing and so was John. What was worse, they couldn't find Yorkie, their small Yorkshire terrier.

Tom and Jean reported the thefts to the police and discovered that the previous day John had been arrested for selling their stolen valuables and other unidentified items to a second-hand dealer. They discovered that he already had a criminal history for fraudulent conversion. He was approached again by the police and questioned about the dog's disappearance but denied any knowledge of its whereabouts.

Distraught, Tom and Jean rang the local council and everyone they could think of and then put an advertisement in the local paper offering a reward. A week later children playing on nearby sand dunes found the body of the dog which had been killed by a heavy blow to the head. Nearby was a blood stained-rock but there was nothing to link the crime to John.

When the case came to court Jean and Tom asked for a male Court

Companion, who subsequently attended court with them over several months because of repeated adjournments. At his trial John pleaded guilty to all the charges and was given two periods of suspended sentences for the Harris case and for other items. The sentence was subject to John's good behaviour and repayment to Jean and Tom of the value of the stolen items at a rate of $200 per month. The breach of trust and protracted court proceedings took a heavy toll on Tom and Jean. Tom developed severe fatigue and left the Church Choir and Jean required medical treatment.

When it was all over their daughter bought them a Cairn Terrier puppy.

In the newsletter of February 1986 Ray recalls:

> For the first five years we were able not only to keep within our income, but we saved a fair bit each year. This was because we were all volunteers and I managed to give considerable time to the oversight of the office. From memory I think we accumulated a reserve of around $18,000.

The first approach to the Attorney-General, Trevor Griffin, in 1980 for financial help must have been difficult for Ray, as indicated by the small amount requested. He explained that he was starting up an organisation to support victims of crime and needed 'a little bit of seed money to start it off'.

Trevor recalls, 'I asked him how much he needed and he said he thought about $500 would be enough. He told me that VSS was essentially driven by volunteers. Ray Whitrod didn't really want to take the credit for initiating it, he was in a sense a catalyst for a number of victims who felt there needed to be a support organisation'.

In view of Ray's strong statements over the years about the need for volunteers to run Victim Support Service, one can imagine he might have felt reluctant to approach anyone in government for a grant so early in the history of the organisation. It says a great deal for his drive and determination that, for nearly five years he was able to run Victim Support Service with so little money. Membership fees were very low: individuals $5, family $5 and pensioners $3. In 1981 a corporate life membership of $250 was introduced which has since been reduced to $215.

Eventually common sense prevailed and annual grant submissions were directed to the Attorney-General's Department. Grants are especially difficult for voluntary organisations to obtain, even today. Money was required to cover operational and publicity expenses involved in urging reform of specific laws. When it became clear that the organisation could not expand while relying solely on volunteers, Ray finally gave in with obvious reluctance. In 1984 he applied to the Commonwealth Employment Service for a grant, seeking assistance to take on an unemployed person through the 'Job Start' scheme.

A small number of the older members still feel the same way that Ray did about employing professional staff. However, the extensive range of services available today has the capacity to assist over 2000 new requests, not mere dozens of people, each year. This is due to all South Australian Governments, regardless of party, continuing to increase funding whenever possible in response to the ongoing changes following the review in 1996.

Ray grumbled in a 1985 newsletter about the yearly cost of keeping a person in prison by comparison with the money spent helping victims to access services. At that time it cost about $15,000 annually to maintain someone in prison. Today it is around $73,000 and rising. He felt that the crime dollar was too heavily weighted in favour of the criminal, a view still prevalent in the community.

By 1986 funding had become a difficult problem. Paul Raymond, the first paid staff member, had been employed in October 1984 and Ray was keen to keep his services but the special allowance had run out and Paul was forced to leave.

Through sheer persistence, a steady annual increase in funding was achieved which, by 1988, was $100,000. However, VSS was notified that, for the1992–3 financial year, the increase would only be in line with the consumer price index. As the demands on services had increased by then, the situation again became difficult. Ray often hid his concerns about finances under a cloak of humour. In June 1982 he wrote of the then Treasurer at VSS:

> Norm Phillips has spent a lifetime in banking and has now retired and is the Treasurer of Flinders Street Baptist Church. He is quite properly a stickler for protocol and I would have Buckley's of tampering with our funds. As well he has a secret weapon. Nobody, but nobody can read his writing, so auditors have to go back twice and always ask for fresh explanations of why the money is wanted.

Later he referred to the next Treasurer, Geoff Pennell, for whom he felt great friendship, as 'Shylock Pennell, our ever grasping Treasurer. As to getting the price of a pie out of the petty cash box, there's even less hope. Geoff Pennell extends to the petty cash the same amount of care he gave to his responsibilities at Elder Smith'. Geoff was also called 'Moneybags Pennell' because of the bags he carried. At the 5th birthday party Ray invited Geoff to cut the cake, making the wry comment, 'I knew he could get more slices out of it than anyone else'.

In 1984 despite the seriousness of the situation, in the last newsletter for the year Ray continued to joke:

> Friends, there I was the other day, full of life, entering the VOCS office when I was unexpectedly confronted by none other than our assiduous friend, Old Money Bags himself. With much effort, the merest flicker of a smile flashed quickly over his countenance. He said, in what was obviously meant to be a jovial tone, 'Raymond, what about omitting all the morbid bits from the next newsletter and just mention the happy things, because it will be near Christmas'.
>
> I was dumbfounded. I could only nod my head in response. I mean everybody but blind Freddy knows that while he claims to be Geoff Pennell who arrived here under the Big Brother movement many years ago, his real name is Geoff Scrooge.

Sadly Geoff Pennell died in 1986 and left a big gap, as he and his wife Ritsie were two of the earliest and staunchest workers. Ritsie continued to help out with newsletter folding for several years when an extra pair of hands was needed.

Brian Curtis

Brian has been a volunteer stalwart on the financial side of VSS for more than ten years. He initially served as auditor and treasurer and after the change in the constitution, continued to oversee the accounts and prepare the financial reports for the VSS Board. After retiring as an accountant he served as Administrator of Wilderness School and later the National Trust of South Australia. In 25 years there have only been four treasurers, all volunteers.

Brian Curtis

In the Newsletter of December 1985 Ray notes that he been advised by the Attorney-General's Department that VSS will be granted $4000, with the balance of $3500 in April 1986, towards the forecast *deficit* of $7500.

Once a significant level of funding from the government had been established during the 1980s, VSS's receipt of grants was guaranteed. In the 1990s, funding increases were modest but steady meeting up to 85 per cent of requirements. Potential private industry sponsors and donors tend to think that governments should be funding services and are therefore reluctant to offer funding. Approaches to business for sponsorship have failed except for two years, 2002–03, when VSS received sponsorship from the Commonwealth Bank which helped pay for the newsletter during this time.

In the latter half of the 1990s a new strategy, designed to access more grants from different sources and special purpose funding, paid off. Small cash reserves were even being held from year to year. The days of Brian Curtis waiting outside the Attorney-General's Department for a cheque to pay the staff were over. The most significant increase was in 2001 when four years of arguing finally convinced Attorney-General Trevor Griffin to finance regional service development. The funding was offered on a three-year trial basis with around a million dollars. It is hoped that this funding will be continued beyond VSS's 25th year. A large bequest from the estate of Thomas Coveny in 2001 facilitated the establishment of an investment plan designed to bring a little more security and financial independence to the organisation.

The Resource Centre at VSS was the focal point for raising donations and 'special celebrations' were identified to acknowledge contributions made to VSS in memory of crime victims Mark Langley and David Barr. Sir James Irwin allowed his name to be used to raise funds from the community and the Irwin family also donated generously.

Victim Support Service – Table of Grants in Dollars	
1980	500
1985	4,000
1986	11,000
1987	62,000
1988	100,000
1989	140,000
1990	226,000
1991	241,000
1992	318,000
1993	353,000
1994	335,000
1995	346,000
1996	416,000
1997	445,000
1998	449,000
1999	499,000
2000	618,000
2001	798,000
2002	830,000
2003	818,000

Sir James (1906–1998) was a prominent architect and one-time Mayor of Adelaide. He was a supportive friend and benefactor of VSS over a long period.

In order to meet the increasing call on services the financial juggling act goes on – but has become less of a tightrope walk.

9. Training, teaching and talks

If each is given a box of tools
A shapeless mass and a book of rules
And each must make 'ere life is done
A stumbling block or stepping stone.

Anon.

Most people need to keep learning, either intentionally or through osmosis. In order to function and stay aware of life's continuing changes, we need to absorb new information daily, which can prove very daunting. For people in the workforce or actively volunteering, there is no other option but to keep learning.

Every organisation, whether business or volunteer-oriented, is expected to provide staff training which includes updating, re-skilling and access to a growing mountain of information. It can also mean taking a hard look at established practices in the light of new information and perhaps doing things in different ways. At VSS, training is necessary for paid staff, Court Companions and other volunteers. One of the strengths of the organisation has always been its willingness to use its relatively few resources to help staff, volunteers and clients, to benefit all who are interested and want to learn more. De-briefing with trained counsellors can also be very important for volunteers and paid staff.

Court Companion training
Court Companions were among the first volunteers at VSS to be given training by police officers and members of the judiciary. They were taught how to conduct themselves in court, to protect their client and shown where to seek help when needed.

As described in more detail in chapter 6, training courses for Court Companions are held annually unless training more volunteers for a special reason has been identified; for example, where there is a need to increase the number of Court Companions in country areas or in anticipation of an upcoming major trial. There tends to be some degree of burnout amongst Court Companions and other people find that family and job pressures change and they are unable to continue. However, many persist for several years and the fact that the majority of Court Companions are retired people helps to maintain continuity and increases the length of service.

To expand awareness of related services and organisations, Court Companions make occasional visits to places of interest such as prisons and courts. The following section describes visits undertaken over past years and some changes may have occurred since.

Court Companion visit to Northfield Women's Prison

On arrival, the information flow commenced immediately and we were introduced to a young, experienced officer with a down-to-earth but compassionate approach. Prisoners are over the age of 18 years, mostly 18 to 26 and are classified as low, medium or high security. Those on remand are accommodated in a separate unit within an area which houses a total of 60 mainstream prisoners.

When a prisoner arrives she is given a comprehensive interview to determine her needs, which may include drug and alcohol treatment, basic education or budget training. About 90 per cent of the women have children, and their primary concern may be worry about their care.

Behaviour and psychiatric problems are noted, as is religion, if any, and diet requirements. Most accommodation is shared, and the prison is usually full, with a maximum capacity of 99 which includes 39 in the Living Skills Unit, which will be discussed in more detail later.

The recidivism rate is 70 per cent and it was suggested by one of the staff that some may feel safer in prison than at home in spite of the restrictions, especially if they are subject to domestic violence.

There are four accommodation wings. Prisoners occupying B Wing have the most privileges and undertake work in the prison, such as in the kitchen and laundry. B Wing includes long- and short-term and remand prisoners. The reception area is housed in C Wing and here women undertake a seven-day observation period when first admitted. D Wing is a special-needs area for those with behaviour difficulties. There are double and single cells and prisoners can watch TV and movies. In A and B wings prisoners are allowed to bring in their own television sets.

The Intervention Unit is staffed with social workers and psychologist case managers. The role of the two social workers is to comfort distressed women and to counsel them. Women are able to attend courses covering a variety of subjects, including domestic violence, drugs and alcohol, literacy and numeracy, victim awareness, behaviour management and quit smoking programs. The prison also has an education officer and a psychiatrist who visits once a week. These professionals are not classified as custodial staff.

The next stop in the prison visit was the Prison Industry Complex which has three functions: to provide a trade and hands-on work experience which may be useful later; to encourage the women to use their skills; and to provide accredited training linked to a domestic trade suitable for employment after release.

Our last call was to the Living Skills area, which accommodates 37 women and at times a small number of babies. An education facility is located on site, with the women having access to computers and a library. Women in the Living Skills Unit are classified as medium to low security and must be drug free. Some of them are permitted to work off site in the final 12 months of their sentence. Children are allowed to visit at weekends and the women have to budget, order and cook food. There is limited provision for some gardening, which is voluntary.

Visits are allowed in the Association Area where TV is available and meetings are held. Members of the staff have a good rapport with the women. The aim is to assist the women to leave prison with more skills than they had on entry and to become law-abiding members of the community.

The opportunity to glimpse the other side of the wire is appreciated by Court Companions who work only with victims.

Visit to Yarrow Place

Yarrow Place is the Rape and Sexual Assault Service, a community offshoot of the Gynaecology Department of the Women's and Children's Hospital, although totally self-contained. The staff consists of a director, social workers, clerical backup and rostered male and female doctors.

The Police Sexual Assault Unit conducts the initial interviews. The slightest penetration by any object and oral sex are both included in the definition of rape. The defence, not the victim, has to prove consent.

Counselling may be necessary for the victim to decide whether to press charges. Only a small percentage of rapes are reported and an even smaller number charged and convicted. There may be fear of the offender, threats, shock, feelings of disempowerment and issues of consent. The reality is that many offenders are known to the victim. The developing interest in victimology – measuring the impact of crime on the victim and on society – as a subject for scientific and psychological study, is relatively recent. It mirrors the awareness, which began to grow in Australia and overseas in the 1970s, of a comparative lack of justice for victims.

At Yarrow Place group programs are provided in addition to one-to-one counselling. Education and training programs are also run for police, doctors, nurses and community educators to increase their understanding and the need for preventive action. Education programs emphasise the risk of accepting drinks from strangers in a pub or nightclub since they can be laced with tasteless drugs with relative ease, a practice which can exacerbate the action of alcohol. The programs also emphasise that friends should look out for each other.

Visits have also been made to Yatala, the Remand Centre and all the city courts.

Training the trainers

It's all true, or ought to be, and more and better besides.

Sir Winston Churchill

These days many professions require ongoing education to maintain registration or keep up to date with new knowledge and technology. In the early days of VSS, Ray Whitrod, familiar with training courses through his experience in the police force, was constantly on the lookout for conferences and opportunities to establish communication with similar organisations.

As described earlier, Ray attended a variety of professional conferences in Australia and overseas, as do other members of VSS staff these days. The interstate victimology conferences served to increase support and co-operation in the early 1980s between victim support groups who were just starting out and finding that attracting members and funding was difficult.

In 1981 Ray describes how he regularly addresses each intake of potential police inspectors, prosecutors and detectives on the role of the victim in the criminal justice system. In that year also he began giving similar lectures to base-grade police, court officials and prison officers attending courses at the former South Australian Institute of Technology (now the University of South Australia).

The overseas conferences at which Ray played a prominent part, put Australia and South Australia in particular, on the victimology map. They facilitated the exchange of information about different services and enabled visits from a wide selection of people, visits which benefited members of VSS, but most particularly victims.

In 1986 Ray spent time learning Indonesian prior to a meeting of the Executive of the World Society of Victimology, of which he was a member. There are many other examples, mostly funded out of his own pocket, using 'Mavis' holiday fund'. From his interviews and writings it is possible to detect a slight feeling of guilt or regret but his patient and supportive wife as he noted in his autobiography, *Before I Sleep*, never complained.

In 1987 a conference was held in Adelaide entitled *Criminal Justice – Towards the 21st Century*. It was a combined activity between the Australian Crime Prevention Council, Offenders' Aid and Rehabilitation Service and the World Society of Victimology. The conference supported separate and combined meetings of the organisations, providing a unique opportunity for a range of people from similar organisations to get together.

Adelaide hosted the 8th International Symposium on Victimology in 1994 which was organised by the Australasian Society of Victimology with the support of the World Society of Victimology, a body affiliated with the United Nations in Geneva. This was the first time such an important conference had been held in the Southern Hemisphere and it was deemed a great success, with 400 delegates and 160 speakers from each of the five continents. In addition to serious reporting, the media reported upon the occasional off-beat item; for example, when a Dutch visitor announced that countries with heavy beer drinkers suffered more crime than those where wine was the preferred tipple!

In 2000 VSS took on the challenge of organising a national conference which ultimately attracted 200 delegates from all states and territories. The title of the conference was *Victims of Crime – Working Together to Improve Services*. The presenters included such dignitaries as the Chief Justice, the Chief Magistrate, the Attorney-General, the Chief Executive of the Justice

Department, the Assistant Commissioner of Police, the Chief Executives of Offenders' Aid and Correctional Services and the Director of Public Prosecutions. During the conference issues and strategies in areas of criminal justice, health and welfare, education, indigenous and multicultural services were discussed. The organisation of the conference was a collaborative effort and provided unique opportunities for future planning and networking.

Over recent years VSS's two chief executives have given numerous conference papers, both in Australia and at international symposia overseas, most recently in New Zealand, the United Kingdom, Canada and South Africa. Counsellors also contributed to interstate conferences. Such representation of VSS and South Australia has helped maintain the organisation's international reputation as a leader in the field.

Counsellors regularly deliver training to university students in law, legal studies, journalism, social work, psychology and to the staff of various health and welfare agencies. An important training activity is undertaken with serving police officers or those who have been newly recruited. This aspect of VSS's work stems from the early days and has been steadily expanded. New training materials have been developed and packaged into high-quality professional training tools.

For nearly ten years VSS has partnered with the police in presenting joint two-day victims of crime courses, which have been extended into regional areas and delivered to hundreds of police officers.

Public talks

Right from the beginning, a significant proportion of Ray Whitrod's effort went into public speaking, largely to attract members and money. Other members, especially Bob Whitington, also undertook what was essentially public education. In 1996–7 a more formal Speakers' Group of volunteers was formed and members will go anywhere at any time – within reason! A speaker's kit had been developed to encourage consistency, accuracy and professionalism in the talks. The number of talks each year varies between 50 to 60, reaching a total audience of up to 1500, not including those given by staff.

Public education

Strategies to reduce the incidence of crime are continually being developed, tested, revised, retained or discarded by police and associated organisations, and VSS has designed or participated in several of these.

Australians, along with other nations who until recently believed they were safe anywhere, especially at home, are losing the 'She'll be right' attitude to self-protection. These days we all lock our cars and houses even when we are still inside! We are advised not to hitchhike or pick up hitchhikers, but some people still do. However, it is necessary to strike a balance between sensible precautions and paranoia.

There are rules for crossing the road and swimming between the flags. In the same way, we are advised how to make our homes, workplaces and ourselves safer. Much of it is common sense but the rules are multiplying and becoming more prescriptive as the number of ways that we can be scared, threatened and hurt, increase.

In 1998 the VSS newsletter published a number of suggestions to minimise the likelihood of having a handbag stolen. This is a very common crime and one where older women are particular targets. A woman may be knocked over and injured as a young person rides past on a bike grabbing the handbag as they go. The suggestions offered include:

1. Put a wallet in an inside or front pocket.

2. Keep a spare set of keys with a neighbour in the event of losing the bag.

3. Carry your money in a small flat bag used for passports around the neck.

4. Don't carry large amounts of money or valuables when going out. If worried about a break-in, rent a small deposit box at a bank.

5. Turn fear into anger.

6. Check your insurance policy for handbag contents loss.

7. Use a 'bum' bag or small backpack instead of a handbag. However, these can be cut from behind, so consider a small bag with a long strap which can be worn across the body with the bag in front.

8. Always report a loss to the police.

In addition, remember your sharpest natural weapons are your elbows, your fingers and your feet – if you are wearing shoes.

Fear of crime

In 1984 Ray drew attention to the following statistics. In Adelaide 14,500 dwellings were broken into, affecting 36,000 people, including Ray himself and wife Mavis! Only 8 per cent of these break-ins were solved. This represented a 24 per cent increase over the previous year and was the equivalent of one in 27 dwellings. (This figure did not include arson, rape, murder or serious assault, which had their own categories.) In 1981 South Australia had the highest rate of burglary of any state or territory. In *The Advertiser* on Friday 5 July 1985, Ray wrote an article headed 'Why Adelaide is the Burglary Capital of Australia'. Ray noted in this article that break-ins affect neighbours and increase the community's fear of crime, especially amongst the 30,000 women and 10,000 men who were over 65 and live alone. Today the figures would be substantially higher, although it is difficult to make comparisons because of changes in legislation and legal definitions (refer chapter 13).

Research has shown that the elderly are less likely to be victims of crime than young adults but it has also shown that the elderly are disproportionately fearful of crime. This fear often results in aged people becoming house-bound, leading to social and health deficits and a life of loneliness.

Studies also indicate that recovery from crime, whether home invasion or personal assault, can depend on the extent of family and social supports, whether the offender is caught and the victim's attitude to the crime. 'I was unlucky' or 'I was lucky', 'It could have been worse' and 'Why did it happen to me?' are all familiar responses. The more help and support a person receives after an incident, the more rapidly they are able to resume outings, social visits and independent shopping.

A woman, whom we'll call Pat, stopped her car at traffic lights and was terrified when a youth jumped into the passenger seat, pushing a knife into her ribs and snarling at her to get out. She found returning to driving very difficult for several months after she got her car back but persisted and eventually recovered her confidence. Pat reports ruefully that she now drives with her car doors locked and hopes never to be in a car fire.

Early in 1989 Ray Whitrod held a meeting with the Commissioner for the Ageing and a member of the Police Research Unit to discuss the problem of fear of crime among senior citizens – although fear affects not only the older age groups. This led to a three-day national conference on the subject later that year. From this combined initiative the Crime Information and

Prevention for the Elderly (CIPE) program began in 1990 with John White as the coordinator.

To launch the program several council areas with a high proportion of retirees were selected, the first at Burnside. The new program was presented as a series of four seminars covering the following topics:

- an introduction to VSS

- current government strategies against crime, such as Neighbourhood Watch

- personal strategies such as self-protection and awareness

- community responsibility and household security.

Brochures were distributed and a time for questions was made available.

A review of the program was conducted the following year, which reported that ten courses had been held with an average of 21 participants and for which there had been a great deal of positive feedback. Three courses had been planned as the program had been extended to cover the metropolitan area and near country areas as well as a large number of additional commitments. These included further talks, displays and debriefing. However, in spite of the apparent success of CIPE, a review was undertaken by a senior police officer from the Office of Crime Statistics. He declared a preference for community-wide crime prevention committees rather than the 'nuts and bolts' of the individual approach. Consequently, government funding was withdrawn in December 1994.

Cartoon – Simon Kneebone

Should Victim Support Service be talking to offenders?

Responses to this issue are likely to be mixed depending on individual points of view and in any case, there are no simple answers to the question. The important issue is increasing the offender's awareness of how their crimes impact on their victims and society generally.

VSS has a policy of supporting the education of offenders in jail and the younger the offender, the more likely it is that the message is received and understood. The causes of crime are complex and to a large degree society-based, but dealing with issues of crime is more than government programs (including prison) for the offenders, it also involves consideration of victims of crime.

Assisting victims to come to terms with the crime which has affected them and their family goes a long way to assist healing. The extent to which this occurs depends on each individual and surprisingly, many are not vindictive even in the worst scenario. A few victims want to meet the perpetrator of the crime against them to ask 'Why?', to receive an apology and an assurance that he or she will never repeat the crime.

There is a huge outcry from the public when a lenient sentence is perceived to be inadequate, but few people respond when a heavy sentence is imposed, except libertarians. This response suits the government's law-and-order campaign, but in fact, the public rarely has all the information, and judges appear to be in the same position at times.

Without doubt there are some crimes, which are so heinous, that incarceration for life seems too lenient an option. On the other hand, most offenders will be released, and unless an attempt is made to educate or re-educate them in jail, they are likely to emerge even more inadequate than when they were locked up.

Some programs have been tried and while it's a question of 'make haste slowly', there is not a great deal of money available. In 1998 the Court Companion group was provided with 'Straight Talk', a program for schools and community groups. During the presentation, two or three selected prisoners, accompanied by an officer from Correctional Services described in graphic detail what it was like to be locked up and lose normal privileges for extensive periods. They were also willing to talk about their own crimes and take questions from the audience.

In spite of the program receiving several years of positive feedback funding was eventually withdrawn. Some time later, another program,

'Just Consequences', took its place but was again slashed in the 2002–03 budget cuts.

There are many social justice boxes in the system and two of them are labelled 'too hard' and 'not enough money'. How long will it take before we get it right and how will we measure success?

Ray Whitrod once made the point that when one is writing or talking about victims of crime, specific experiences should be referred to. Talking in general terms often means that the audience is unable to relate to the victims. It is important that an audience is able to put themselves in a similar situation – which, of course, they hope will never happen. The difficulty lies in treading the fine line between empathetic reporting or speaking and sensationalism.

10. The newsletter

The most significant achievements of human endeavour
are the products of human cooperation.

John Oliphant, Social Worker
8th International Victimology Conference 1994

Picking up an anticipated, well-reviewed book can be compared with the start of an adventure. Preparing to research the history of Victim Support Service by reading the two recently bound copies of the first twenty years of newsletters, was such an adventure. For nearly ten years they were written wholly by Ray directly onto a typewriter. Probably as a result of his many years of writing police reports, his typing skills were excellent and his style was conversational, enthusiastic and personal. In later years he reduced his input and others took over the editing role.

So personal were they, that while at all times professional, repeated reading indicates a lot about the man and how he is reacting to events. In the early days Ray often referred to victims by their first name and followed their progress with practical sympathy and concern, while reporting their experiences in the newsletters over several months.

Among those were the Bell family whose daughter was abducted from her bedroom, the Ratcliff family, 'Julie', 'Karen' and many more. Ray provided ongoing support over many years and was upset if he felt he had neglected anyone.

The House on the Hill

It was a Wednesday and John usually took the family's German Shepherd, Tara, with him on the day he saw clients in the Barossa Valley. On this occasion he was alone. The previous week she had been found dead, poisoned by something the vet was unable to identify. So both John and Anne were in low spirits. Anne waved him goodbye and then saw the children onto the school bus and went inside to start her chores. The house was the last at the top of the hill in a new subdivision. It was a very quiet area during the day and Anne often worked to loud music.

Glancing at the old grandfather clock, which chimed every quarter of an hour, Anne saw that it was just after nine. As she turned on the radio, she felt spooked, as if someone was near her. God! She'd forgotten to lock up. The house was split-level and she ran up the short flight of stairs to the front door as an intruder pushed past, and strong hands grabbed Anne from behind as she stood in shock.

He jerked her arms back, causing sharp pain in her shoulders, at the same time covering her mouth with masking tape. Then he swung her around bringing her hands to the front so that she saw the balaclava concealing his face. Shock turned to anger and Anne began struggling but she couldn't prevent him looping a rough rope over her wrists and then around her body, trying to tie it round her waist. Only partially successful, he knocked her down and tried to twist the rope around her ankles.

He was tall and strong but Anne was gym-fit and pulled away grunting and snorting behind the tape. She dragged him down the stairs to the living area, where she lashed out with her foot. He cracked his fist across her head, temporarily blinding her. She collapsed on the lounge, stunned and terrified. Again he tried to tie her feet with the rope, having succeeded in wrapping it round her waist.

Anne kicked out again, winding him. 'You bloody bitch', he gasped. They fought and struggled up and down the stairs for what seemed an eternity. Finally he managed to drag her into a bedroom and threw her on the bed. 'Now we'll see who's winning'.

She could feel her strength fading and with a mighty effort she lifted her tied, bleeding hands and pulled off the balaclava, scratching his face in the process, a face she would never forget.

He leapt back with a shout of pain and a stream of curses. His hair was flat with sweat and the scratches began oozing. Picking up the end of the rope he thrashed it across her legs in frustration, gasping with fatigue.

Then, without another word turned and left. Anne heard the front door slam as she lay on the bed exhausted, feeling as if every bone in her arms and legs had cracked.

Unaware of the clock during her ordeal she counted eleven chimes. They had been fighting for nearly two hours! For another hour or so she drifted in and out of consciousness. Eventually she managed to pull off the masking tape, the pain nothing compared with that in the rest of her body. She couldn't free her hands, which were numb, swollen and purple but managed to get to the phone and with difficulty rang the police before collapsing on the floor. When they arrived Anne burst into tears.

The police asked a few questions while waiting for the ambulance to arrive and she was able to express the thoughts which were whizzing around in her head. Hardly any words had been spoken but her attacker had a distinct, gruff voice and he had probably been observing the routine of the household for some time.

'Thank heavens I was wearing jeans', Anne said and burst into tears again. The police officer urged her to relax and reassured her that she was safe now, although he knew it would be many years before she would ever feel safe again.

Anne spent several days in hospital and went home covered with bruises to a seesaw nightmare of sharp, red fear, chronic fatigue and insomnia. John gave up his country visits. Two weeks later the offender was arrested in the process of repeating the attack on a woman in a nearby house.

The trial processes of arraignment, adjournments, giving evidence and appeals went on for months. Anne had a particularly difficult time, as the defence attempted to minimise the seriousness of the attack because she hadn't been raped and she had the feeling that the jury, mainly women, wasn't sympathetic either. She was very grateful for the Court Companion who stayed with her for every twist and turn. Eventually there was the relief of a stiff prison sentence.

Two years later, the family returned home one Saturday evening after watching a football match and were slumped in front of the TV with chicken and chips, half watching the news. The new German Shepherd, Shay, lay at their feet. Suddenly, Anne screamed and stood up, her plate of food falling to the floor. Her attacker's face was on the screen with the announcement that he had escaped.

Two sleepless weeks later he was caught. Anne is very strong, mentally and physically but this time her husband agreed – they would sell up and move house.

The early newsletters were chatty, friendly letters sharing information. In fact, such was Ray's enthusiasm and commitment that many were 12 pages long. As far as this book is concerned, the difficulty has been in deciding what to include and what to leave out since the detail is so extensive. He often began with 'Dear friends' and signed off 'Your Friend', or just 'Ray' and the writing was often light and amusing. The format, name and logos have changed over the years.

Title of newsletters

From August 1979 until June 1982 the newsletter masthead read *Victims of Crime Service Newsletter*. From August 1982 until August 1991 the publication was called *VOCS News*. From December 1991 until December 1993 it was called *VOX*, and between February 1994 and December 1997 it was *VOCS Quarterly* then *Victim Support Service Quarterly* until 1999. In 2000 the newsletter was renamed *Victim's Voice*.

Ray was keen to share his wins and losses, and older members often commented on how they looked forward to receiving the newsletters. From 1986 a few professional advertisements appeared in the newsletter which assisted with the cost of production. They were usually from lawyers associated with the organisation.

In 1988 Ray reduced his contribution to four pages and staff reports made up the remainder. When he relinquished his role as Chairman of the Council he stopped writing for the newsletter and the format changed. Of necessity the newsletters became shorter and more concise, conveying fact not opinion and were less colourful as a result. Other editors included Bob Whitington and David Pemberthy who took over in 1994 and adopted a magazine format. Over the years many individuals have made their mark on the newsletter, particularly those in administration whose technical and design skills are very much appreciated.

Now in the twenty-first century, new technology permits a wealth of information to be presented in colourful format on the internet at VSS's attractive and easily manipulated website www.victimsa.org. In addition, professionally prepared and interesting quarterly newsletters continue to be sent to members.

The typical newsletter has many roles, which include keeping members up to date with new legislation, seeking support for a particular campaign, sharing victim stories and poetry, providing information about meetings and introducing new members of staff. They also provide information for victims, contact with the media through opinion items and a forum for other points of view. These days each issue is carefully planned by a committee of staff and volunteers and is the main vehicle for public statements and general publicity.

In 2004 readership was estimated to be over 10,000 through the 3000 copies which are circulated. Newsletters are distributed to members as well as to police stations, libraries, members of parliament, Neighbourhood Watch groups, many local councils and to other health and welfare services. The news and views of VSS continue to reach a wide audience and even travel overseas.

The logos

The logos have also changed over 25 years. The first one was semi-abstract which could be interpreted as two figures waving. It was designed by Bob Keay and lasted until August 1982.

First logo

This was followed by a more figurative design commissioned by Bob Malin showing one figure with a comforting arm across the shoulders of a second person who could be weeping.

Variations of this logo, such as enclosing it within a circle, were used until the name change to VSS in 1996 was followed by the creation of a totally new logo in February 1997.

Second logo

It was designed by Andrew Davies who described it as evolving from the need to provide an immediately recognisable, contemporary expression of the service. Commenting on the new logo, Michael Dawson wrote: 'There is a continuity with the old logo through the stylised heads and arms which link our past with our future'. The new logo was selected to highlight a more modern approach, a new name and new bright, positive colours.

Third logo – current

11. Delivering the goods

To our patrons, advocates, defenders, activists, encouragers, Paul, Olive, Mary, the remaining galley slaves and I.

Ray Whitrod, August 1985

Staffing

If you have a job without aggravations, you don't have a job.

Malcolm Forbes, author

Well, that's one point of view, to which not all would subscribe, although it is the reality for many people. Others thrive on challenges and problems, and as mentioned in earlier chapters, Ray Whitrod used his enormous energy and strong personality to confront all the difficulties which life kept presenting to him. He was committed to encouraging volunteers to undertake all of the work at Victim Support Service – starting with Court Companions and office helpers. As we have seen, at the outset there was no money for paid staff, and from 1979 until 1984, all administration and management functions were performed by volunteers.

By December 1983 Ray was virtually forced into agreeing to the formation of a finance committee. The aim was for this committee to develop a budget and identify funds for a small staff, particularly an executive officer. Even then, he presented argument and counter-argument when he felt under pressure. It's not always clear why Ray was often so vehemently opposed to the idea of paid staff, but it may have been related to his need to be independent of red tape after so many years serving in different police forces.

He once wrote:

> There is an inbred resistance to change in bureaucracies and the utili-
> sation of obsolete arguments and out-of-date data only makes it easier
> for them to resist reforming proposals.

Perhaps the irony that he also was resisting change escaped him,
although in the previous comment he was referring to changes to the law.
However, by April 1984 Ray Whitrod had written:

> I must confess that at long last (hoorah) I have come to accept the
> inevitability of our having to employ a coordinator full time in VOC's
> office. The rapid expansion of our sister group in Victoria, VOCAL,
> after they had taken this step compared to their fairly slow beginning
> has convinced me we must do likewise.

For Ray, accepting office staff was the first conciliatory gesture, but
social workers were altogether a different animal and that took longer. From
time to time Ray made very derogatory remarks about them, including a
particularly scathing attack in 1986, which, if examined closely appears to be
defensive in response to comments from others that Victim Support Service
could not be taken seriously because the organisation did not employ
'professionals', that is, paid staff. In April 1986 he wrote in a newsletter:

> It seems to me that some of you think I am a little uptight about the
> need to preserve the original idea of VOCS as a voluntary, self-help,
> independent group of victims wishing to offer friendship and support
> to others in distress. Perhaps I am. Bob [Whitington] and I have been
> selling this concept now for six years and perhaps we are a trifle
> inflexible. *But we are still committed to it.*

Administration

There are days when it takes all you have got just to keep up with the losers.

Robert Orben, author

When a grant became available from the Commonwealth Employment Service
in 1984, **Paul Raymond** became the first paid employee at Victim Support
Service. Ray was gracious enough to be generous in his praise of
the administrative work Paul undertook, the courses he attended and the

submissions he wrote. He even suggested that Paul had the potential to take up an executive role if the money lasted, which it didn't, and Paul left after two years.

On his departure he wrote to Ray, 'I take this opportunity to thank VOCS Council and particularly yourself for the assistance and respect shown to me over these two years'.

Ray described Paul as: 'a very gentle person with a splendid sense of humour and a quick mind. I will miss him and so will a number of others'. Ray was revealing his soft side! A group of Court Companions went into recess until Paul could be replaced because they felt so vulnerable without professional support.

Other employees from the early years include **Des House** who was employed full time in January 1988 and who stayed nearly three years. As Des was studying social work he was offered a dual role – he was a part-time counsellor during the time Ray Whitrod was undergoing his first hip replacement and part-time administrator. Des enjoyed working as part of a team with other staff and remembers that one of his most interesting jobs was to mount a public display at Old Parliament House on the work of Victim Support Service.

The Workload

Well, if I called the wrong number, why did you answer the phone?

James Thurber, satirist 1894–1961

The aims of Victim Support Service have always had to be balanced against the available finance and the staff to meet the needs of clients. While there have been a number of occasions when the rate of staff turnover has been alarming, there has always been a consistent core who have provided the necessary continuity of service and philosophy. The reasons for the high turnover rate are largely attributable to many staff being seconded from other organisations, on work experience, or only available until grant money ran out.

The social work component in particular can be quite stressful but the rewards very fulfilling. On occasions crime victims say that it's a job they couldn't do themselves.

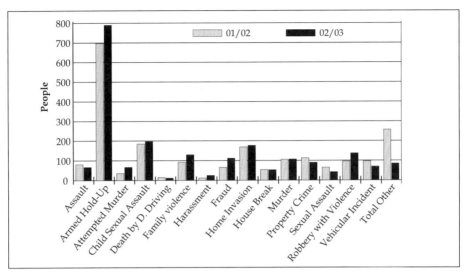

VSS Crime Statistics. First contact by type of crime.

Social workers

Even though it is sometimes hard to hear the terrible experiences our clients go through it is a privilege to be a small part of their survival and recovery. It is rewarding and inspiring to watch people draw on their courage and inner strengths as they learn to live with the trauma and losses they have experienced.

Audrey Stratton, Victim Support Service Social Worker 2002

The first social workers to be employed were **Jan McClelland** and **Kate Hannaford**, hired by Harold Weir while Ray was away in 1988. Kate was seconded for 12 months from Correctional Services and Jan, who was hired to fill in for four weeks, stayed more than two years.

In her interview Jan recalls being given a free rein by Harold to be innovative. She started the Armed Hold-up Support Group following an incident at the Festival Centre. She also recalls the tension at Victim Support Service as the result of being the first professional working in a fiercely protective volunteer organisation. This was not a problem while Harold was around, but when Ray returned to work he wanted Jan and Kate to 'move on'. Jan recalls that Harold warned Ray: 'You will have the whole social work profession down on your head and I wouldn't risk that if I were you'. Ray backed down.

Ray later softened his attitude to social workers when he began to appreciate their contribution to all-round client care and realised that Victim Support Service could not expand without them. In 1990 **John Oliphant** was the fourth social worker to be employed, promoted to Senior Social Worker in 1992 when **Kate Baxter** returned to New South Wales after 12 months.

John stayed five years and found the work challenging and rewarding, particularly admiring the Victim Support Service philosophy of never turning away anyone who needed help. Ray was on the selection panel and later told John he was appointed because he clearly cared about victims and their rights. In his interview John Oliphant comments:

John Oliphant

> I think there's a misconception sometimes that Ray was anti-professional, that he didn't want professionals involved in the organi-sation. I don't think that is true from my experience and contact with him at that time. He was against certain things that professionals sometimes did and sometimes stood for but he was actually very supportive of professionals if he felt that they had their heart in the right place.

John Oliphant remarked that he had noted a passion and commitment among the volunteers and social workers in relation to the victims and their issues, which he had never come across before, or since. He liked the culture and philosophy of Victim Support Service, which included volunteers and paid staff working alongside each other and being equally appre-ciated. This cooperative spirit continues today and is one of the great strengths of Victim Support Service.

Many other staff came and went for short periods. A social worker who stayed longer than usual and made a big impact was **Rebecca Abbott**. In her interview Rebecca remembers the good and the not-so-good times.

She began work for the organisation in

Rebecca Abbott

January 1994 after working as a student on a three-month placement, which she describes as wonderful work experience. Rebecca says she was nurtured and carefully supervised in those early days, especially by **Katrina Dee** who worked at Victim Support Service for four years and made a great contribution to the women's groups. When Rebecca started as a fully qualified professional, she 'was thrown in at the deep end' in the new position of Intake Social Worker, the initial contact for new clients, a role she really enjoyed. For Rebecca the balance between one-on-one contact with a client and the various groups she facilitated was ideal. She noted that some clients naturally progressed from individual counselling to the groups where they could share similar experiences, and most people knew when they were ready and what they wanted.

During the difficult times of the mid-1990s Rebecca found the tensions among the staff a burden which exacerbated the inherent stress of the job. She coped by burying herself in work and was relieved when changes finally eventuated. 'It was very good timing for the organisation to be reviewed', she said of the 1996 review.

Rebecca also commented that she had enjoyed working with the Court Companions as their facilitator and recognised that, without volunteers, the organisation couldn't operate at the current level. 'The workload is so huge that, without them, the paid staff could not cope.' Clients and staff alike appreciated Rebecca's cheerful, calm manner and missed her when she made her next career move in 2000, after six years. Victim Support Service has been fortunate over the years in attracting social workers with the skills and commitment of Rebecca Abbott.

David Kerr

A social worker who has become an invaluable contributor to the high standards of both client and staff care at Victim Support Service is David Kerr. In a newsletter profile he described himself as a 'refugee from Keynesian economics turned social worker'. After completing a degree in Economics at Flinders University in the mid-1970s he undertook a post-graduate degree in social administration. To help pay his way he worked in a wide range of part-time jobs from

David Kerr

strawberry picking to brickie's labourer. His first post-graduate jobs included working with the Education Department at Elizabeth before moving to the Crisis Care Unit which was then managed by Andrew Paterson. From there he helped set up a Crisis Care Unit in Perth before joining Victim Support Service in 1992. He has gathered additional skills along the way and is now Manager, Professional Services at Victim Support Service, while retaining a caseload.

David commented that he still enjoys the work because: 'I am totally captivated by the capacity for the human mind and spirit to bear up under extreme adversity; there is so much to admire here and so much to learn'. His quiet, approachable manner and sense of humour are greatly appreciated by clients and staff.

Responding to clients

Over recent years the social workers have constantly searched for ways of minimising the wait for services – as the demand continues to grow. Their work model is one of flexibility, open to new ideas and characterised by regular reviews.

In 1990 Andrew Paterson, then Executive Director described social work at VSS as follows:

> We become closely involved with clients, living through the experience with them, offering support through the early stages of shock and bewilderment, listening and encouraging the victim to talk… Much of our work involves explaining processes and advocating before systems and bureaucrats. 'Counselling' is not giving advice, it is the highly skilled task of helping victims take back responsibility for their own lives.

At the time of writing, the counselling teams are divided into the 'Long-Term Team' and the 'Intake Team'. Members of the former may each have caseloads of up to 35 clients and there is no time limit or fee for assistance – 'as long as the client needs it'. To help reduce the pressure, the duty counsellors may take over clients they assess as having short-term needs. In addition, all social workers have other responsibilities, such as supervision of special client groups, organising particular promotions, maintaining links with associated organisations and supervising student placements. Many clients who are accepted for counselling find that previously suppressed, but unrelated or complex traumas may emerge in this safe counselling environment.

Consideration also needs to be given to the social workers themselves who, in undertaking counselling work with clients to ameliorate their trauma, run the risk themselves of 'acquiring trauma'. Appropriate de-briefing and other workplace occupational health and safety measures are always in place.

Librarian

The Library has always been a unique and valuable resource and was started by Ray Whitrod with donated texts and articles. In the early 1990s Andrew Paterson brought in two students to organise and formalise the collection. Various volunteer 'librarians' came and went until 1999 when the Attorney-General responded to VSS's request for specific funds to improve the Library.

By employing a fully qualified librarian, **Fiona Hemstock**, for one day a week, the organisation was demonstrating that the Library/Resource Centre is an important part of core business and no longer an adjunct or addendum to the services. Many students, volunteers, staff from many organisations and clients now use the Resource Centre, which has over 2000 catalogued items, including many counselling and self-help materials suitable for clients.

Chief executives

A sense of humour is part of the art of leadership, of getting along with people, of getting things done.

Dwight D. Eisenhower 1890–1969

In the newsletter of April 1989 Ray announced his withdrawal as Executive Director. Later in the year he had his third hip replacement – 'third time lucky' – and the position was advertised. The job went to **Andrew Paterson** who had met Ray in the early years when he was responsible for setting up the Crisis Care Unit in South Australia.

In his interview for this book Andrew refers to being selected by Ray, who managed to have Andrew transferred from a government to a non-government

Andrew Paterson   position without loss of privileges but on a reduced salary. His brief was to 'professionalise Victim Support Service without antagonising the volunteers'.

Andrew has 'hundreds of fond memories' but acknowledges that only a year later he and Ray were experiencing 'areas of conflict'. One of these revolved around Andrew buying some new furniture to give a more welcoming impression to clients attending the depressing facilities in Flinders Street. He described the offices as having 'carpet that was taped up with masking tape, broken windows that hadn't been fixed, the lift from hell and the darkest, dingiest staircase in the history of architecture'. While Ray raged at the cost: 'This is not an up-market government department', the situation was saved when the Victim Support Service Council decided a move was necessary to relieve the serious overcrowding.

Another difficulty arose in April 1995 when Andrew Paterson was invited by the then Minister for Correctional Services to join the Prisoner Assessment Committee as the inaugural Victim Support Service representative. Andrew had not consulted Council first and describes the discussion with them as 'energetic to say the least'. One issue related to a general reluctance by members for Victim Support Service to be seen having anything at all to do with criminals. As we have seen this attitude has gradually changed.

It is now generally accepted that by representing victims, Victim Support Service can influence change within the justice system and participate in reforms. Membership of the Prisoner Assessment Committee by the VSS CEO has continued since then, and Victim Support Service is perceived as making a significant contribution to policy regarding prisoner management (refer chapter 14).

Happy times included the big celebration at the Stamford Grand Hotel, Glenelg, to mark Ray's retirement to which both Andrew and the senior social worker, David Kerr, wore kilts. Despite these lighter moments, the conflict between Andrew and Ray became more intense: 'Ray and I did not end up on good terms at all'. The personality clashes and financial problems eventually led, in 1995, to Andrew Paterson leaving Victim Support Service to take up the position of General Manager at Mobilong Prison where he stayed for a year. Today, Andrew accords Ray a great deal of credit for his energy, commitment and sheer intellectual talent.

For the next six months David Kerr took over the reins as Acting Executive Director, his calm, unruffled manner helping to keep everything running smoothly by 'taking one day at a time'! Around this time John Oliphant and Katrina Dee also left. David has written about this difficult period as follows:

> There were no professional or administrative procedures and there was no policy manual. We all held our breath around payday. On one occasion the Treasurer waited at the cashier's office in the Attorney-General's Department to collect the grant money and put it in the bank immediately to pay the salaries due in six days time.
>
> Throughout this period the organisation maintained a very high media and public profile. It was well respected and well known in the professional and wider communities.
>
> At the end of this period a very serious split occurred within the staff group. This spilled over into Council and the volunteer group. The upshot was that three of the senior staff departed within months of each other. For five months we hobbled along. We had three or four social worker staff (depending on the month). From this group was drawn an acting executive director, there was no senior social worker. It was a time of very high stress and the organisation teetered on the brink of extinction. The only reason we survived financially was because our salary bill had been halved.

Michael Dawson

Michael Dawson

There was a general sigh of relief in 1996 when Michael Dawson was appointed as the new CEO, and Victim Support Service continues to benefit from his training, experience and energy. Michael had previously worked in management consulting and human services as a psychologist, both in the government and private sectors.

His work has covered a wide range of areas, including educationally disadvantaged children, people with disabilities, Aboriginal groups and the unemployed. His interest in criminal justice was fuelled by a review he undertook of strategic directions in the Northern Territory Correctional Services Department and, in South Australia, his involvement as a consultant in recruiting the first team of Youth Justice

Coordinators for the Family Conference Team. He has developed a strategic approach in re-building relationships in financial and human resource management, and having a written plan to follow and monitor progress.

Michael's excellent negotiating skills and friendly personality have succeeded in putting Victim Support Service back on track, revitalised so that once again it is a strong and energetic organisation. The 'new look' included the move to shopfront premises at 11 Halifax Street. The bright and welcoming reception area forms an appropriate backdrop to a modern well-run organisation. Michael says he was lucky to be in the right place at the right time.

With David Kerr's support Michael has tried to attract a psychologist to join the social workers in the counselling team. Several psychology students have completed professional placements at VSS and joined as paid counsellors for short periods. The social workers enjoyed the input from a different profession and are keen to establish a multi-disciplinary team.

The Board of Management

One volunteer is worth two pressed men.

18th century proverb

Last but by no means least are the members of the Board (previously the Council) who, not unlike company directors of a business – without the salaries and perks – are also volunteers, perhaps not as well known to clients or volunteers as those staff in 'front of house' but nevertheless always working conscientiously in the background. At the same time they are dependent on the work of the paid staff in order to make informed decisions about the direction of the organisation. The Board is a necessary and valuable supervising part of the triumvirate of clients, staff and volunteers, and the group of people who, in law, carry the greatest responsibility.

The first Council meeting was held on the 18 June 1984, the year Victim Support Service was incorporated, and comprised many of the early personalities, with Ray as the Chairman, Barrie Hibbert as Deputy Chairman and Geoff Pennell as Treasurer. Other members included Sir James Irwin, Mary Maitland and Bob Whitington. Over the years many other volunteers have served in this worthy role.

It is a difficult task to try to select a few names out of so many, and tedious to mention them all, so only those names which are attached to specific events have been recalled in this narrative. It should be emphasised however, that Victim Support Service is very grateful to all who have made a contribution and to those who continue to do so. A number of outstanding people have given their time and effort over the years and Victim Support Service and the community owe them a great deal.

Elke Pfau was a different kind of volunteer. Born in Germany, she was a serving police officer in the Victims of Crime Branch (as it was then known) when she joined Victim Support Service in 1989. She became Chairperson in 1995 until after the review in 1996 when **Tony Pederick** took over. Elke contributed substantially to the establishment of a good working relationship between VSS and the police force, especially with the Police Victim Contact Officers.

From the very first meetings, Council minutes and the minutes of the Executive were produced, and they make very dry reading. There are dates, names and the actions agreed to but absolutely no detail to give colour and shape to the debates which must have ensued. This is not unusual in all types of organisations where confidentiality is essential, and by following the Constitution, a legal document, the decision-making is protected.

Elke Pfau refers in her interview to the difficult time at Victim Support Service around the period of 1995–96 when decisions made by the Board were often immediately conveyed to staff and volunteers, leading to dissension and causing dissatisfaction. (Rosemary Huxter recalls that minutes were often circulated to the staff). All that changed with the government review of Victim Support Service in 1995, after which new standards and changes were put in place. Elke still feels that Victim Support Service leads the way in victim services.

The main items considered in the early years include approving conference leave and a recommendation that the Council should comprise one-third women. Another 1980s recommendation was that Victim Support Service needed more trained volunteers and fewer social workers and should avoid 'peripheral issues'. What those issues were is not spelled out and the senior citizen who moved that motion shall remain anonymous! So full were the Board members' lives, that for some years meetings were held at 7.30 in the morning! In 1991 this time was changed to 4.30 in the afternoon to enable an elected solicitor to attend. Since then the meetings have remained at that time.

The Executive minutes are even more cryptic. For example in August 1990, it is minuted that, in future, Andrew Paterson (then the Executive

Director) must report to Ray Whitrod (Chairman) before taking leave. One could speculate on the discussion which led up to that pronouncement! On the other hand, it may simply have been a matter of convenience and communication, although cracks were beginning to appear in their relationship at this time.

More recently **Russell Jamison** joined the Board in 1996, as Chairperson from 1999 until 2003. A Life Member of Victim Support Service and born in America, Russell began his working life as a social worker in Boston after completing a Bachelor of Arts degree. Early in the 1970s he decided to emigrate to Australia and study law, completing his degree at the University of Melbourne and commencing practice in Adelaide in 1975. Russell is quoted as saying that his main concern with the judicial system is the large number of different courts with their own forms and rules. This results in an immense load of paperwork, increasing costs beyond the availability of most people.

Following the major review in 1996, the constitution was changed to require a Board of four elected and three appointed members. The new Board reflects the need for governance to oversee a million-dollar enterprise holding expertise in legal issues, accounting, criminal justice practice, media and business to bring a balance of skills as well as a passion for victim issues.

While it is clear that the Board has more responsibility and less of the drama and occasional fun of the day-to-day work, their role is to provide oversight of the planning and financial management. It is the legal entity to which the staff are responsible and accountable.

Regional services

As the word spread, demand for Court Companions came from country areas. The training of volunteers from Mount Gambier, the Riverland, Whyalla and Port Augusta gathered momentum in the early 1990s. In 1993 the first two Aboriginal Court Companions received their training certificates and regional services are now available across South Australia.

Commencing in July 2001 after years of urging by the Board, the Attorney-General awarded VSS a three-year grant to expand regional services for victims of crime in the five regional areas of Port Augusta, Port Pirie, Port Lincoln, the Riverland and the South East. A tremendous effort was required and a regional services coordinator was appointed, **John Cobb**. VSS now provides services on a statewide basis, although some communities are still served by a needs-based, outreach service.

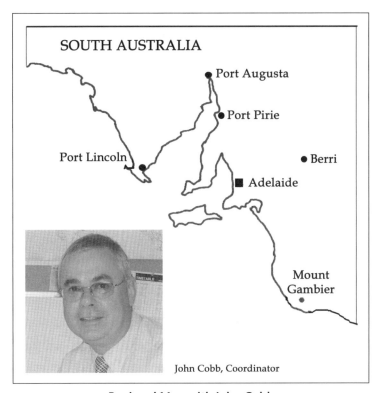

Regional Map with John Cobb

In addition to working as Court Companions, volunteer country staff also use the public speaker's kit to deliver talks to local communities in the same way as their city counterparts.

For the sake of expediency there is an emphasis in regional areas on working with established community services. In this way working partnerships are developed. These tap into existing organisations which assist the local communities; for example, Lifeline South East (SA) Inc at Mount Gambier and in Port Lincoln, Eyre Peninsula Women's and Children's Support Centre Inc.

The following quote is taken from the 2001–02 annual report on regional services.

Services in all regions include the following provisions:

- *A part-time Local Area Coordinator to provide information, counselling, practical advice and support to victims.*

- *Volunteers who provide practical assistance; for example, Court Companion, help with Victim Impact Statements, public speaking and administration.*

- *Locally based office, interview and group-work accommodation which is also available to prosecution witnesses when they are waiting to give evidence in court. The Courts Administration Authority is providing us with accommodation next to the court in Port Pirie and a room in the court at Mount Gambier.*

- *A Local Victims Liaison Committee, consisting of key stakeholders and service providers, to support the work of the Local Area Coordinator and to reinforce local 'ownership' of the Service.*

- *Training and education of professional workers and the community aimed at promoting awareness and shared responsibility for preventing crime and assisting victims to recover.*

- *Contributions to campaigns and projects that inform the community and contribute to strategies and policies which enhance community safety.*

- *Assistance with the implementation of the Declaration of Principles Governing Treatment of Victims in the Criminal Justice System.*

- *The provision of services which are accessible to all sectors of society.*

We have formal partnerships with locally based organisations to provide services as our agents.

Local communities have responded positively and enthusiastically to the introduction of regional services and are working in close collaboration with us to ensure success. There are examples of our activities encouraging other positive developments, including South Australia Police who are endeavouring to provide additional Victim Contact Officer resources, and crime prevention committees establishing dedicated sub-groups to address victim issues' (John Cobb, Regional Services Coordinator 2002).

For 25 years countless thousands of hours have been dedicated to Victim Support Service – from volunteers folding newsletters and acting as Board members to dedicated professional staff. This is surely an outcome of which to be proud.

12. Special groups

Total grief is like a minefield. Not knowing when one will touch the tripwire.

Sylvia Townsend Warner, 1893-1975

Many of us are likely to become victims of crime during our lifetime to a greater or lesser extent. It may be a snatched handbag, a stolen car or a home invasion. We all hope that it won't get worse than that, but remember how shocked you were and how vulnerable you felt?

Twenty-five years before the government catchcry 'Don't be alarmed, be alert!' punctuated our daily lives, VSS was providing support and reaching out to its clients and members. Support groups designed to meet specific needs relating to different crimes have emerged, both in Australia and overseas. It is a sad fact that the list is expanding, but occasionally groups do close down if there is no further demand or other services take over. One of Victim Support Service's great strengths is its ability to adapt to changing circumstances and client needs. The therapeutic groups conducted at VSS are unique in Australia and comprehensively described in a paper by staff member Rosalind Jamison for a conference in 2003.

The Moving Forward Women's Group

In October 1989, eight women who had been victims of crime took part in the first eight-week Women's Support Group program facilitated by social worker Kate Baxter and assisted by Libby Zada, on secondment from the Queen Elizabeth Sexual Assault Clinic. The second course took place early the following year and the demand for follow-up meetings was so strong that the Ongoing Women's Support Group was formed, which met every six weeks. The group meetings enable women to share their common experiences of grief, anger and lack of power and foster mutual support, the ability to make decisions and reduce the deep sense of isolation that many victims feel.

Now renamed the Moving Forward Women's Group, it still consists of an eight-week course facilitated by two social workers from VSS. The feedback includes comments such as, 'I realise I'm not crazy', 'I get support and understanding' and 'I found the group very relaxing'. These group gatherings continue to be active, the processes and operational models changing as appropriate.

Quiet Lies

The fluttering leaves
On the Autumn trees
With deep rich shades to behold,
Tell many tales
Through rain and gales
Of sadness due tenfold.
Dark tired eyes
Strong wrenching cries
Of pain held deep within,
A falsehood here and there
The promise that they care
The slyness of an ogre's grin.
Your trusting heart
To be ripped apart
And searched by demon eyes,
Take what you need
And leave me to bleed
I'm used to your quiet lies.

Tricia Lee

After Child Trauma Group

In 1991 the Domestic Violence Unit was established within the South Australian police force, with ten officers appointed to investigate child abuse. In the same year The Special Mum's Group was formed for mothers whose children had been sexually abused. In the early days the members of the group took turns to meet in each other's homes once a fortnight. In 1997 a 10-week course conducted in VSS offices was developed for these parents and facilitated by a social worker. An ongoing support group was also developed for those who required it, using a flexible meeting format, usually every six weeks. The support group continues to meet and assists new members through courses conducted by two VSS social workers. The group is now referred to as the ACT group.

A Child Abuse Working Party was convened in 1997 and members spent a very busy year raising public awareness of the poor deal which child victims receive in court. With little effort made to ensure that courts are child-friendly, children are often overlooked or considered unreliable witnesses. For this reason it is often difficult to ensure that male offenders acknowledge their crime and receive punishment for it. The stated aim of the working party was:

> … to find ways of improving the current system, so that victims of child sexual abuse and their families are dealt with in a fair and dignified manner at a level that the victim understands.

In spite of all the effort, the media largely ignored mail-outs, personal approaches to members of parliament, a seminar, petitions with nearly 5000 names and a rally in Victoria Square. Some felt it was a disappointing outcome for such a substantial effort. Nevertheless, a few changes have taken place since then, although they have been a long time coming and the situation is still far from ideal (refer chapter 14).

April Two Nineteen Ninety Six

My daughter was only four years old
When the sexual abuse was first disclosed
She told me all the ins and outs
Of what daddy did when I wasn't about
It was a secret, she couldn't tell

Cause if she did, she'd go straight to hell
But she told mummy and was praised
resoundingly
Daddy's very naughty and he needs counselling
But daddy denies it, so what do you do?
Nothing apparently, because of her youth
She has no voice in our justice system
She's only five and they will not listen.

Jan Stevenson

Families Against Senseless Tragedy

In 1990 Peter Ottoway and Nigel James set out to achieve more prompt and comprehensive support for families and friends affected by road accident trauma – by organising an independent support group with the acronym FAST. It was independent of, but supported by VSS, which assisted with writing submissions over several years. Judi Rea also worked long and hard in this area. A protest group which aims to change what is considered inadequate legislation or procedures can be a constructive way for people to work through their grief and help others, and many groups both here and overseas have commenced in this way.

In brief, FAST wanted a central, consistent focal point to supply immediate coordinated information, professional counselling, links to other resources and ongoing support as required. The following eight years were to prove more difficult than these pioneers could have imagined, involving representation to a wide range of services seeking support in principle or practical assistance, and necessitated endless meetings and negotiation with South Australia Police, government departments, members of parliament, community and private organisations.

Persistent lobbying led to the formation of a working party within the Attorney-General's Department where all stakeholders (including VSS) were represented. A report was produced in November 1991. Among the recommendations was the provision of grief training for staff in agencies dealing directly with families, such as SGIC third party insurance, the Coroner's Office, police and others.

Police needed a comprehensive information pamphlet to hand to families and an excellent handbook is now available. Families also needed to be notified of court dates and other formal matters at a time when they were having difficulty coping. More funding to VSS was recommended, as the organisation would be expected to supply the long-term support to the increasing number of families who would be referred.

Other suggestions both within and outside the terms of reference were made. The item which FAST considered crucially important was also that which took longest to implement – a Victim Contact Officer (VCO) within the Major Crash Investigation Section of South Australia Police. Besides being an essential element in initiating further support services, such a position is in line with the practice of having a VCO in other relevant police divisions, such as Major Crime. At first, police representatives would only consider the provision of such a service in cases of 'murder by motor vehicle' of which there were two or three a year in South Australia, and 'when charges were pending', which didn't go far enough for FAST. Discussions were still taking place late in 1998 and minutes of a meeting at this time noted: 'The trauma to families of fatal motor vehicle crashes is the same as murder victims. Reasons different. Results [the] same'.

In March 1999 a discussion paper listed the gains which had been made to date, the major exception being the provision of a Victim Contact Officer. Persistence paid off and in April 2000 the position became a permanent addition to the Major Crash Section and continues to this day. FAST provides an excellent example of the way dedicated individuals can make a significant difference to so many other lives.

Having achieved most of their aims, FAST has been disbanded, with a high level of burnout being experienced by some of the members, although individuals will still speak to newly bereaved families if requested.

The Armed Hold-up Support Group

This group was inaugurated in November 1994 following a report about the impact of this crime on the victims and an alarming increase in hold-ups. VSS offers specialist advice to employers (including Australia Post in 1989) in preparing staff for a traumatic experience such as this and recovery assistance to employees who have been affected. Subsequently this group became known as the Armed Hold-up and Home Invasion Group so that victims in the latter category could be included.

Most armed robberies take 3 minutes or less!

Paula was thinking as she sipped her mid-morning coffee how much she enjoyed her job as a teller at the Building Society. She liked meeting the customers but was looking forward to the weekend because today was Friday, and just like any other Friday ...

Paula jumped and splashed her coffee as the door was pushed open so hard that it hit the wall. A tall figure in a blue tracksuit and black balaclava leapt onto the counter and pushed a canvas bag at her. She could only stare at the gun he was holding which suddenly discharged with a loud crack. Sure she was shot, Paula froze and waited for the pain, her thoughts flashing to her children.

'Come on, you know what to do', the hard voice jarred her into action. Like a robot she began to follow his instructions, explaining in a small voice that she would have to go to the adjacent counter because where she was standing, the drawers held only stationery supplies.

His thin, rigid figure stayed calm as Paula filled the bag but he was standing so close she could smell his aftershave. In a detached way, as time seemed to have slowed down, Paula wondered if he'd just had a shower. When the bag was full the robber jumped back over the counter, knocking over her name sign. Then reality hit and she pressed the alarm button. Paula slowly realised that three other people in the room were frozen in positions of shock and the hands on the clock seemed not to have moved.

When the police had finished interviewing and dusting for finger prints, Paula left to pick up her girls from school and on the way home tried to tell them, in a light-hearted way, what had happened. The following Monday Paula drove to work feeling sick and struggled for twelve months to come to terms with the mixture of anxiety and health problems. Back in the 1980s there were no counselling sessions to de-brief staff, or automatic glass screens to protect them.

Almost a year to the day Paula had an 'anniversary reaction' – a panic attack resulting from unresolved stress. She quit her job and didn't work for eight years as the after-effects put pressure on her marriage and family. Eventually Paula found a job in a nursing home where only banging doors make her tense. She still regrets that she had no counselling, as she believes it would have speeded her recovery. And there are times when she contemplates the year the multi-convicted robber may be released.

That particular Building Society still doesn't have glass screens.

Adapted from a VSS newsletter feature

Home invasion

Previously referred to as housebreaking or burglary, home invasion is still an all too common crime. Each week the local papers report the 'break-ins' which occurred in the district with the implication that no one was home at the time. The new term, 'home invasion' sounds (and is) more sinister and expresses how we feel when our castle, our safe place, is invaded. The meaning, however, can have different interpretations when described by the police, media or the public.

The South Australia Police definition is 'A person … enters a home for the purpose of committing an offence and deliberately seeks out the occupant'. That is the scary part, deliberate confrontation. Forced entry, use or threat of violence, demands and removal of property amount to 'armed robbery in the home'.

This description appears to be an escalation from breaking a window in an empty house to gaining entry and forcing a shed door to steal a bike, and it is. In South Australia, 'robbery with violence' under section 158 of the *Criminal Law Consolidation Act 1935* carries a penalty of life imprisonment. And there is some provision for self-defence 'on reasonable grounds' in the face of violence or threatened violence.

The trauma becomes more substantial if personal and irreplaceable items are stolen, or there is gratuitous vandalism. Whatever the circumstances, victims react in different ways, as with any crime. Victims may experience anger, confusion and disbelief, and many people seek counselling and support.

At the annual general meeting of VSS in 1990, the Attorney-General, Trevor Griffin remarked, in discussing the role of VSS in meeting community requirements, 'The need to minimise the risk of being a victim will become even more important. Self-defence, self-protection and protection of one's property will assume a more significant role'. His emphasis was on education and changing the culture to better appreciate the needs of victims. This was at a time when there was a great deal of publicity about the rights of the criminal.

Articles, statistics and advocacy in *Victims' Voice* were important in the reform process and on 19 October 1999 *The Advertiser* published an article by Miles Kemp under the heading 'Pressure Forces Move for New Laws'. It stated that Trevor Griffin had bowed to public pressure and announced new laws 'to crack down on home invasion'. Trevor proposed three alternatives and VSS was consulted. VSS held firm against the unrestrained public demand for heavier punishment and sought a more rational analysis of the problems and tailored solutions.

Around the same time, encouraged by the media, a 79-year-old woman led a highly emotive and angry rally on the steps of Parliament House and presented a petition signed by 73,000 people demanding tougher laws for perpetrators of home invasion.

For those who are concerned, a great deal of information is available to assist people to make their home safe without turning it into a prison. The local police station and Neighbourhood Watch are good starting points. Self-defence classes and a cool head go a long way and even a small dog which barks when someone knocks on the door, could be worth the effort of feeding and exercising, with companionship a bonus.

At the time of writing, a woman of 77 was challenged at night in her home. When the intruder produced a knife she punched him in the face and he dropped it and ran. Rightly, the police warn the public not to be heroes but one can't help feeling a certain satisfaction at such bravery. Of course, resistance can just as easily exacerbate such a dangerous situation.

Robbery with violence

This refers to a crime committed in public, usually by someone unknown to you. It includes snatching a handbag, an ATM hold-up, demands for money and threats with or without an obvious weapon. Shock may render you 'frozen', confused and fearful and more symptoms may follow, but recovery *will* occur over time, as you receive appropriate care and are assisted in coming to terms with the experience.

Homicide Victims Support Group

Lynette Nitschke launched this group at the 8th International Victimology Conference held in Adelaide in 1994, following the murder of her daughter Alison by a fellow university student. Always independent, the group now operates under the umbrella of Anglicare at the Loss and Grief Centre in Prospect.

Andrew Paterson was instrumental in helping to establish and support the group and VSS continued to offer help and accommodation until the growing numbers required that it move to larger premises. There appears to have been significant benefit in having two quite different groups raising issues and advocating for victims of crime. In the event of such an horrific crime as murder, the process of grief management, resolution and recovery, or at least being able to move on in one's life, is complex and protracted and outside this discussion.

Life after Threat, Terror and Endangerment

In 2001 an ongoing, open support group – which may be unique in Australia – was established for those who had experienced any form of life-threatening crime. The new group encompasses victims who had been part of the armed hold-up and home invasion groups and replaces those groups. Many of the issues raised here have the potential to be extremely confronting and require resolution after the group meeting. Launched in 2002, it is the only group available for both male and female clients and is facilitated by a male and a female counsellor. One of the facilitators has worked with STTARS (Survivors of Torture and Trauma Assistance and Rehabilitation Service) and there may be some points of comparison, although the circumstances are different.

The quiet achievers

My world was ripped apart on 17 August 1994 when the most horrendous tragedy occurred. My father, Bent Sorenson and his fiancée, Karin Murphy, were brutally murdered in their home. My family and I have endured immense pain, sorrow, grief, frustration and anger, which have left deep scars within us. Our lives will never be the same again.

Despite our tragic circumstances, we have met some wonderful people who have played important roles in our healing process. One of these people was a Court Companion, who accompanied my family throughout the whole court proceedings, from the committal hearings to the sentencing. The Victim Support Service provides training and assistance to Court Companions, who are a group of dedicated, hard-working volunteers.

My family was extremely grateful to have the strong, committed and yet tireless, support of a Court Companion during our ordeal in court. Our Court Companion explained all the court procedures as they unfolded, as this was very foreign and overwhelming to us. He sat patiently with us through the endless hours of waiting outside courtrooms. He was very caring and considerate of our needs.

We appreciated his perceptiveness in realising the times when we needed to be alone with our thoughts. He gave us moral support and smiles *when we needed it and even shared a few laughs to brush away the tension.*

I believe that Court Companions are the 'quiet achievers' behind the Victim Support Service. Thank you to our special Court Companion and congratulations to all Court Companions on doing such a great job.

Birgitte Sorensen

For more information ...

In this section we have considered a few of the most common crimes and an overview of the support which is available.

A list of brochures and fact sheets on these subjects, published by VSS in several languages, can be found in the Resource Centre or on the website (refer appendix 4).

13. The legal scene –

or when do you need a lawyer?

To no one will we sell, or deny, or delay, right or justice.

Magna Carta, *clause 40*

Think about it! How many times do we grumble that there are too many rules and regulations? From birth to death we are governed in every aspect of our lives, except that birth happens and death is inevitable. In between, we are subject to 'You *can* buy a car but you may not drive it until … and don't forget to keep to the left'. And 'You may apply to build a house but first you must …' or 'You can keep a dog in the city but it must be …' and so on.

Of course we need laws to provide a safe and democratic community and avoid general chaos but how do we learn which laws apply to us? Some of them (especially those based on ethical considerations) are part of our culture which we are taught as we grow up or learn by trial and error. We learn to read and research information from government and independent organisations and we accept that filling in forms is part of life.

What happens if we can't read and don't care about our community as long as our own needs are met? How do we react if we are caught breaking a rule or inadvertently become a victim of a broken rule? In either case we are thrown abruptly out of our comfort and knowledge zones. We find ourselves inside a complex web of laws and circumstances, which we don't understand and which can be overwhelming. If the situation is serious enough we may need a lawyer to guide us through the maze. And if we can't afford a lawyer what do we do then? Did you know that there is no automatic legal representation for victims in a trial? You might expect the prosecutor to be on your side but don't count on it. He or she is there to represent the community and you may be a small cog in a very big wheel. Victim witnesses often talk about feeling left out of the loop.

On a more sophisticated level we may become involved in or aware of laws with which we don't agree and feel they need changing but as individuals we can't normally achieve this. Many more new laws are created or amended than repealed.

The second primary aim of VSS, after caring for victims of crime, is to make justice equitable and available to all victims. For 25 years VSS has worked hard, arguing persistently for change where needed, writing submissions and making representations to both sides of parliament in South Australia, to the Commonwealth Government and even to the United Nations. Achieving legislative review requires knowledge, energy, endurance, commitment and a great deal of time. Working to change, improve or remove laws deemed outdated or unfair has always received a high priority at VSS. In 1982 Ray Whitrod wrote:

> … goodwill has never been enough. Knowledge is required if our arguments are not to be dismissed out of hand, as much of the work of uninformed do-gooders can cause more harm than benefit to the community. Voluntary organisations can suffer from the over-enthusiasm of its members who may give advice to enquirers which is incorrect. It is not done deliberately but in ignorance of the correct procedure.'

This chapter reviews some of the most important legal issues which have impacted on victims and with which VSS has been involved. Changes can have a long lead time between idea and implementation. New legislation usually starts as a draft bill, which may be released for community discussion and consultation as well as being debated in parliament. When the bill is passed by a vote, the Governor gives assent. During the next stage clauses will be negotiated to enable the development of regulations which assist interpretation and implementation.

The following descriptions of acts and legal procedures may appear both complicated and less interesting than the rest of this book. Every effort has been made to highlight only the most important issues in each piece of legislation mentioned, but if this isn't an area which interests you, then skip to the last chapter!

Right of appeal

Established by the Crown in 1981, this was one of the first pieces of legislative change supported strongly by VSS – usually because the sentence was perceived to be inappropriate, or too light. VSS argued that, in this area, South Australia was out of step with the rest of Australia.

The unsworn statement

Under this practice defendants who had given unsworn evidence could not be cross-examined on it. This loophole meant that presumed lies and evasions could not be challenged, a situation which had been a source of public frustration for many years. Thus it became an early target for the Truro group and in the VSS newsletter of October 1980 it was nominated as the subject for concentrated submissions and objections to the government during 1981.

The unsworn statement dates back to medieval times when illiterate or people with an intellectual disability were often tortured to extract confessions which meant that many statements were untrue or couldn't be relied upon. There had also been opposition to its use in other Western countries and it was abolished in Britain in 1982. In 1983 the South Australian Attorney-General, Chris Sumner, admitted that there had been community opposition when he decided not to remove the unsworn statement from the judicial process. To counter its effect, he argued, prosecutors could produce witnesses to refute claims made by the defendant, a practice which promoted the argument that witnesses could be dead or too frightened to appear. Finally, after many years of campaigning, changes to the *Evidence Act 1929* including the abolition of the unsworn statement, were passed in South Australia on 1 November 1985.

The Right to Silence

This anomaly had a similar legislative resonance to that of the unsworn statement. In all Australian states an accused person has the right to testify or not, as he or she chooses, and a co-accused has the right to make adverse comment on that failure to testify. However, whether the judge or prosecutor can comment on a failure to testify varies across states. In South Australia only the prosecutor is prohibited from commenting on an accused refusing to testify. Similar situations occur in other countries; for example, the United State's Fifth Amendment in their Bill of Rights.

The Bail Act 1985

In December 1984 Ray Whitrod reported on a bill before Parliament to facilitate the granting of bail to suspects under arrest or those on remand. Bail
authorities rarely asked victims whether they would feel vulnerable to
threats or at physical risk. VSS's plea for change was lost by one vote in the
Legislative Council.

However, during renewed debate on the act in 1987, the Shadow
Attorney-General, Trevor Griffin, was able to include an amendment that
victims should be consulted about bail conditions. In 1994 there was again legislative change whereby *primary* consideration was to be given to the idea that
a victim may have, or perceive to have, a need for physical protection.

The Declaration of Victims' Rights

On 30 October 1985 this important policy statement was accepted in State
Parliament – six years to the day from the start of the campaign. The battle for
recognition of victims' rights had been fought over many years, and indeed,
it had been pointed out by a Canadian academic, Professor Irvin Waller,
that no member country of the United Nations, including Australia, had
dignified the needs of victims of crime.

Around this time an article written by Ray Whitrod had appeared in *The
Advertiser* entitled 'Redressing the imbalance'. Ray had written:

> For too long the rehabilitation of the criminal has taken precedence
> over the interests of a victim who might still be suffering physically,
> emotionally or financially long after the offender has been returned to
> society!

Criminal Injuries Compensation Act 1978

> *The three R's are remorse, repentance and restitution.*
>
> Ray Whitrod

Victims were concerned that financial compensation was often difficult to
obtain and the cost of legal advice was, and is, high. Both these issues were
the subjects of approaches to the government.

In 1983 the statutory maximum compensation for murder cases was
$10,000. At the time this compared unfavourably with other states when
maximum compensation in Queensland was $38,000, West Australia $15,000,

Victoria $21,600 and New South Wales $15,000. There are two sources of compensation through the courts: firstly, compensation or restitution from the offender is determined in court during a criminal sentence proceeding and most often made for property offences. The reality is that it can be very difficult to extract recompense from convicted people, many of whom may have few assets. Victims of an offence at a public venue may be compensated by the operator's public liability insurance.

Criminal Assets Confiscation Act 1996

This act remedied the situation described in the previous section by enabling an offender's property to be seized and the money paid into the Criminal Injuries Compensation Fund, which is administered by the Crown Solicitor. In one of the first such orders, a judge directed that a BMW car worth about $15,000 be forfeited to the Crown. It should be noted that confiscation of assets does not equate to a direct benefit for a victim.

Harold Weir remarked in an interview in 1999:

> My experience with prisoners is that they forget all about what they have done and the crimes committed. I am very much in favour of some forcible means whereby prisoners are the ones who make the reparation or contribute to the reparation.

The *Criminal Injuries Compensation Act 1969* offers the alternative pathway towards receiving monetary compensation and recognition of injury. Most applications for compensation are heard in the District Court. However victims may negotiate with the Crown Solicitor's office without a court appearance, usually for amounts less than $10, 000, even when the offender is unknown. Since early 1985 the scheme has been supported by the **Criminal Injuries Compensation Fund** which sources money from a proportion of fines, proceeds of assets obtained by crime, a 'victim's levy' on fines or expiations paid in South Australia and backed up from general revenue. A percentage of fines is paid into the Compensation Fund, with VSS receiving an allocation.

> In October 1985 the Attorney-General, Chris Sumner, in an attempt to redress a number of the perceived shortcomings of the 1978 act, amended the act by adding the following, as reported in the VSS newsletter:

- *For grief consequent upon death (without showing injury)*

- *But spouse and parents only*

- *Confiscation of assets to pay compensation (not from drugs).*

The act was amended again in 1987 with the maximum payout increased from $10,000 to $20,000; after 1 September 1990 the maximum became $50,000.

The current situation is that all applications for compensation are received in the Criminal Injuries Division of the District Court and the application must be made within three years of the date of the offence. The exception is children who can claim anytime up to 21 years. In the case of dependants claiming for the death of a family member, the claim must be made within twelve months of the death. The amount awarded may be calculated from claims for injury which include pain and suffering, financial loss, psychological suffering and grief, and funeral expenses. There are exclusions and limits depending on the victim's contributory behaviour, and the act excludes claims arising from motor vehicle accidents which can be claimed under the appropriate compulsory third party insurance.

In the mid-1980s an interesting comparison in England arose in relation to victim compensation. The Director of the English National Association of Victims Support Schemes, Helen Reeves, reported that, in the year ended March 1986, the organisation had received 39,697 claims and had resolved 29,965 of them. There was an accumulated backlog of 51,490 unresolved applications, and the awards made amounted to (the equivalent amount at that time) of $100 million. The cost and numbers seem mind-boggling to us in South Australia but apart from the significant difference in population, the figures indicate what we know and regret, that crime is a growth industry.

The Victim Impact Statement

The legislation covering this issue, enacted in 1988, was a big step towards equality within the justice system for the victim vis-a-vis the rights which have long been in place for the offender. This is an important component of restorative justice (refer chapter 14).

Impact statements are presented to a court following a conviction or a guilty plea. Initially they were prepared by the investigating police officers who described the crime and its impact on the victim and the family of the victim. From 1992 a procedure was adopted which utilised a more verbatim report, relying on direct input and/or written responses from the victim in relation to the perceived impact of the crime on them. By 1998 statements could be read out in court.

These are now used by judges in all jurisdictions, and in 1993 in the case of the *Crown v Thompson*, a significant victory for victims was realised when Judge Legoe, in his sentencing remarks, included written statements from the parents and brother of 18-year-old Alison Nitschke. The VSS newsletter described the 'watershed for victims' as a hollow victory for the parents when the 18-year sentence translated to a non-parole period of 10 years. This occurred before 'truth in sentencing' legislation.

However, the occasion marked some progress which would enable victims to read their own statements in court or have someone of their choice to do it for them.

The key proposals in the VSS submission to the Review of Victims of Crime had included:

- improved dissemination of information

- more explicit information about the option of a victim impact statement being an open letter to the court

- better education about the option of victims to talk to the court or read the statement

- removal of the possibility of the victim being cross-examined by the court

- introduction of audiotape or video link options for presenting the victim impact statement.

The *Young Offender's Act 1993*

Before the passing of the *Young Offender's Act 1993* a number of calls for reform of the juvenile justice system were made in South Australia. For example, in 1990 Kingsley Newman, the Senior Judge for 18 years in South Australia's Children's Court instigated reforms in the juvenile justice system. (In 1860 Adelaide had the first Juvenile Court in the *world*). He wrote a paper calling for changes to the juvenile aid panels and outlined new options, which consisted of a balance between accountability, community protection and rehabilitation. The act resulted from the identification of the need for family conferences and formal and informal cautions. At this time the Juvenile Court became the Youth Court.

The act sets out different stages in making youth accountable for transgressions against the community and therefore the law. In the case of the first offence or what is deemed low-level offending, there are three stages of increasing severity.

1. An informal police caution which can be an 'on the spot' warning, is included in the patrol log and can be used in future Youth Court appearances.

2. A formal caution at a police station which can include penalties such as an apology to the victim, compensation and community work, depending on the severity of the offence or failure to heed earlier warnings. An official record is kept.

3. Attendance at a family conference. A youth justice coordinator runs these in the event that the offence is considered not serious enough for the Youth Court. Also present are the offender, his/her parents, the youth police officer and the victim. A Court Companion may accompany the victim if requested, or the Court Companion may go alone to represent the victim if required. The penalties are similar to stage two, with the victim or their representative having input.

More serious offences are referred to the Youth Court for juveniles aged between ten and 18, except in the case of homicide which is automatically heard by the Supreme Court. A youth found guilty of a serious offence can be sentenced in a similar way to an adult. If they need imprisonment, boys and girls may be detained at the Magill Training Centre and older boys will be housed securely at Cavan.

Protection for vulnerable witnesses

This amendment to the *Evidence Act 1929* came into effect on 1 September 1993. A vulnerable witness is defined as someone aged under 16 or over 75, or intellectually disabled, or a victim of sexual abuse, or at some special disadvantage, such as a victim of domestic violence.

Changes made through an amendment to this act include the provision of closed circuit television to enable a witness to give evidence in a room separate from the court, or a screen to obscure the witness's view of the defendant. An additional variation to the act covers the provision of a person to accompany the witness. These changes all seem to specify perfectly reasonable requirements but unfortunately were not previously enshrined in law, and followed requests from many victims who found the experience of giving evidence very traumatic when in view of the defendant. However, even today, these methods of protection may not be granted automatically.

Domestic Violence Act 1994

In 1994 the *Domestic Violence Act* enabled the police, under certain conditions, to serve restraining orders on members of the defendant's family. A section covering common assault was added which allows a more substantial penalty in the case of assault on a family member.

Domestic violence is a tragic and destructive crime often perpetrated against the less powerful in our society and often hidden, but potentially deadly. We may only hear about the ultimate manifestation when someone is killed, usually the woman. We react with shock and horror then it is forgotten – submerged beneath our busy lives. Do we stop to think about what led to that appalling situation? Where are the children and how are they coping?

Violence in the home takes many forms, financial deprivation, humiliation, as well as physical and sexual abuse. The woman may feel shame, experience low self-esteem and believe it is *all* her fault. And what effect does this have on the next generation? Children may be intimidated, fearful and unable to concentrate at school. Drugs and alcohol may compound the problems. Domestic violence takes place at all levels of society.

Why don't we care more, why don't we help? Community spirit still seems to be alive and well in rural areas but less so in big towns and cities where it is likely to be couched in terms of 'getting involved' or 'interfering'. Would *you* ring a neighbour whose husband often yelled and swore at her and the children in public, to check if she was all right?

In a shopping mall would you step between a toddler and the woman who is about to fell him with a large bunch of keys? Would you approach a young couple fighting on a winter beach when she is crying and half the size of the man? Would you knock on the door of an elderly neighbour you hadn't seen for a few days? If you casually touched a colleague's arm at work and she flinched would you suddenly realise she always wore long sleeves? If you asked a gentle question and she denied your suspicions, would you think, 'Oh, well, it's not my business'?

True, some things are better than years ago. There are women's refuges, divorce is easier, and single parents can link into support systems, but poverty and loneliness can follow and lead to depression. Children get out of control and express their frustration and anger through violence and the cycle starts all over again. Consider the proposition that offenders are often victims first.

The Stalker Bill 1994 (*Criminal Law Consolidation Act – Stalking*)

Defining stalking in law is difficult. Each state has similar descriptions with small differences, South Australia's being the most precise. The law states that there must be at least two occasions where it can be shown that there is *intent* to cause serious apprehension, harm or fear.

As 'pursuit' in many Western cultures may appear to constitute a declaration of love or at least attraction, when does pursuit become criminal stalking? When the victim becomes intimidated and has reason to believe the behaviour is intended to cause fear. This is often the case when the stalker makes sure the victim is aware of his/her presence. The additional charge of carrying an offensive weapon seriously increases the penalty.

In 1999 South Australia had the greatest number of reported stalking offences in the country. A victim of two years stalking by her ex-husband writes: 'It makes me realise how alone women are in these types of situations. To others it may not seem terribly dramatic but the emotional scars and fears are very real to me. I can hear grass grow now, and I am tired of living in my own personal prison ...'

Himself

The woman was in her 40s, small in build, single and quietly spoken. Twelve months earlier she had agreed that a man she had met at a club, whom she often referred to as 'Himself' and who had taken an interest in her, could move into her house. At first he treated her with consideration, until she lent him money and he refused to repay it.

He spent increasing amounts of time at the pub and hit her when she complained. After six months she told him to leave and his reply was, 'Get lost'. His out-of-hearing nickname changed to 'Bullyboy'. A hostage situation developed one night and neighbours called the police in response to loud shouting and banging. The police tried to talk Himself out of the house but eventually forced their way in and released the woman from the bedroom. The man was evicted, bound over to keep the peace and told to stay away.

The woman went to court to take out a restraining order and asked for a Court Companion to keep her company as she was afraid to face the offender on her own. When a Court Companion was assigned, she and the woman met beforehand for a cup of coffee to get acquainted. The woman, who had difficulty admitting that she was a victim because she blamed herself, told how Himself continually beat her and was now stalking her. She couldn't sleep at night and had lost a lot of weight.

The victim and the Court Companion made their way to the court but in spite of many anxious glances, Himself failed to turn up to the hearing. The magistrate adjourned the hearing and another date was set two weeks ahead to give Bullyboy a chance to attend. The Court Companion realised later that she never did hear his real name.

The day prior to the second court hearing, the woman rang Victim Support Service to cancel the Court Companion. Himself had met her in the street and promised her that he had turned over a new leaf. He would drive her down to the court the next day so that she could withdraw the application for a restraining order. She said she was sure she would be all right now and thanks anyway!

A small column in the print media on 24 August 2003 reported that stalking is on the rise in South Australia, although few cases reach the court. According to the Office of Crime Statistics and Research, between 1995 and 1999, nearly 1300 cases were reported to the police, of which only 13 offenders were convicted. Of 349 recent cases only four went to court and all charges were dismissed.

It is clear that the crime is difficult to prosecute because, by the time the police arrive, there is only a distressed victim; the offender has taken off and witnesses may not want to come forward, if there are any. However, these figures must be heart-breaking to those women who fear for their safety and even their life.

Truth in sentencing

Other new legal activity in 1993–94 included provision for the actual length of time an offender spent in prison vis-a-vis the sentence. This had long been a sore point in the community, which considered that the way the length of a sentence was calculated was too complicated and there were too many loopholes which could reduce an expected 'head sentence'. An explanatory illustration from the VSS newsletter of May 1994 describes the conundrum:

> The defendant was sentenced to 12 years imprisonment with a non-parole period of 9 years but with remissions for good behaviour, he will probably be released within 6 years and he could be placed on home detention for 3 years.

The newsletter noted that remissions could also result from overcrowding and industrial action.

Back in 1983 Ray reported that the Australian Law Reform Commission produced powerful arguments recommending that parole should be abolished for federal offences. The commission argued that parole promotes indeterminate and uncertain punishment, assumes that conduct in jail predicts conduct when back in the community, that a long initial sentence is unlikely to be served and that the exact length depends on administrative decisions made in secret.

On the subject of secrecy, Ray had reported in the January 1983 newsletter on changes to government policy. Attorney-General Trevor Griffin had announced that, in the future, the government would publish details of people whose sentences had been remitted or pardoned. There had been 50 such cases in 1982 and Ray had said, 'I am very much against secret decisions made in our name [the community] unless there are valid reasons'.

Victim Support Service has long argued that sentences should reflect the intention of punishment expected by victims and the wider community. In addition, the issues involved in sentencing and parole should be clear and easily understood.

The truth in sentencing changes overhauled laws which had been operating in South Australia since 1988 and included:

- Remission has been abolished and home detention as an option for violent criminals has been removed.

- The non-parole period has been established as the minimum period served by a prisoner.

- Those serving a sentence of five years or more will have to apply to the Parole Board for release at the expiry of their non-parole period. They will also have to demonstrate that they have behaved well and sought to improve themselves while in jail by undertaking activities designated in individual programs.

- For the first time, victims of crime will be given an opportunity to make submissions to the Parole Board.

- The police will be able to make submissions.

Victims of Crime Register

Parole and its associated issues of fear and vulnerability have long been a problem for victims who had felt relatively safe when they knew the offender was locked up. In a 1982 newsletter Ray reported that: 'Some progress had been made in resolving the undue secrecy on parole release'. Victims could be notified of releases from prison, which may affect them, but only on the day the release occurs!

Victim Support Service and others persisted in re-visiting the subject at every opportunity, with eventual success. By 1996 'registered victims' were entitled, under the provisions of the *Correctional Services Act 1982*, to access information concerning the perpetrator which included:

- The name and address of the correctional institution where the prisoner is living

- Details of any transfer from one institution to another

- Details of sentence(s) of imprisonment the prisoner is liable to serve

- The date the prisoner is likely to be released for any reason (bail, leave of absence, home detention and parole)

- Details of escape from custody.

A victim can apply to the Department of Correctional Services which will supply the registration forms. All the applicant's details are confidential to the Parole Board, a situation which enables the victim to make a 'submission of opinion' when the prisoner makes an application for parole. The victim can also be notified of pre-release programs and can supply details of their concerns if necessary.

*　　*　　*　　*

We have taken a very superficial look at some of the laws which may be relevant to victims of crime, whether they've had a bike stolen or been the subject of a severe assault. One of the most important roles of VSS is to review, debate, support or challenge the constantly changing amendments to legislation which impact on victims or the wider community. For more information go to www.lawhandbook.sa.gov.au or the Attorney-General's website at www.justice.sa.gov.au

The number of requests for help from the public each year to VSS in Adelaide and the regional offices exceeds 2000, or about 50 per week. This is still only a fraction of the injuries suffered, so what else is needed?

14. Where we are – and where do we go from here?

*It is always wise to look ahead, but difficult to look
farther than you can see.*

Sir Winston Churchill

The work of a small group of parents, whose rosy expectations for their children turned to tragedy with their brutal deaths, has been transformed, to become today a leading victim support agency whose integrity and standards are unique.

Those parents fought back and supported one another, motivating members of the community and government to take action on their behalf. Over the last 25 years the organisation as we know it today has become an outstanding memorial to the lost children and testament to the courage of those first parents. There have been gains and setbacks over that period, but today's professional and volunteer staff are every bit as committed and courageous as the first group of pioneers in 1979.

Much has been learned and methods have changed, but as life becomes more complex and challenging, the Victim Support Service has grown into a comprehensive and innovative model of assistance and advocacy for victims of crime in South Australia and a prototype for similar organisations interstate and overseas.

There have been major reviews in the past (refer chapter 4), and now there are regular three-year strategic plans developed for discussion and implementation. Recent changes and plans for the future include a database of client information to facilitate better information and research, a client feedback/evaluation process and procedures for the protection of counselling case notes for sexual assault victims having to give evidence. Membership by VSS of the Parole Board to represent the victim's point of view is being discussed, as well as financial provision for assisting Aboriginal clients, migrants who have survived torture and persecution, and a VSS-based homicide worker.

For VSS the most significant event in recent years was the appointment in 1996 of Michael Dawson as Chief Executive Officer. He arrived at a time of severe financial difficulties and low staff morale. Just as Ray Whitrod was the right man for the job in 1979, so Michael has proved to be just what VSS needs in a new era.

Michael and the Board feel strongly that a non-government, independent organisation, which nevertheless requires government money to survive and expand, should be businesslike and accountable in all areas of its operation. The present CEO's management approach encourages staff to be independently creative while working as a team. He has built a friendly environment where clients feel welcome, and where professional and volunteer staff work well together, which was not always the case.

The Chief Executive Officer is the main, but not the only public face of VSS and Michael Dawson capably presents the organisation's point of view in his dealings with the media, the government and the public. Without shirking from the difficult issues he is always courteous and professional in his approach – qualities that Ray Whitrod insisted were essential in representing the needs of victim support.

The organisation has sought to reduce its reliance on a 'single personality' culture. A positive strategy has been established to empower staff and volunteers and to encourage the profile and influence of VSS to grow. Spreading the 'power' makes for a stronger organisation which will withstand party politics and encourage a team approach. The strength of a group is much greater than its component parts.

Restorative justice

There have been a number of major changes in recent years, both in the justice system and the development of victimology. One of the most interesting legal concepts is restorative justice or 'trying to make it right for every one'. Everyone includes the community, the victim, close family and friends and the offender. At least part of the rationale is that, as the pressure on courts increases, new ways are needed to divert the offender before he/she gets there. Primarily however, it is a way to involve victims in the legal process and facilitate recovery.

The notion of restorative justice began to emerge in the mid-1990s with an emphasis on including the victim in the offender-retribution loop. From reading about or listening to any number of victims' stories we can see that almost no one is satisfied with legal outcomes, even today. Many victims believe we have a legal system but not a justice system.

In the case of serious crimes a victim's life will never be the same. Thus the community has a responsibility to attempt everything possible to help victims heal and come to terms with the consequences of crime. It is not only the immediate family who are affected but friends, suburbs, towns and ultimately, society itself. Crime is expensive from the start, and individual costs may be ongoing for years. Fear is catching and insurance costs continue to rise.

Restorative justice aims to restore the victim, the community and the offender. Why, you may ask, should we bother about the offender? Let him/her go to hell! There are many reasons, but if only from pure self-interest, we should care. Many offenders follow a path of increasingly serious crime which suggests that the punishment they receive (or don't receive) is not helping them or benefiting the community.

In 2000–01, 254,598 serious offences (excluding traffic) were reported to police, that is, 697 a day. Of those who appeared in a Magistrate's Court, 70 per cent had offended previously and 30 per cent had more than ten convictions. Of those appearing in the Supreme Court, 80 per cent had previous offences. This is just in South Australia!

Keep in mind that only 50 per cent of crimes are reported to the police. The situation is therefore even grimmer than at first appears. So perhaps it is not surprising that the public is generally sceptical of a system which tends to be convoluted and drawn-out, has frequent court delays, cannot return stolen property, appears to hand out unbalanced sentences and cares more about the offender than the victim. Scepticism often turns into outright anger and severe depression.

So do we have anything to lose by being less adversarial and more constructive?

The victim could be formally involved in any stage of the process – investigative, judicial or corrective. This already occurs in family conferences where the young offender and the victim of crime have a chance to meet, an experience which the offender often finds more difficult than an appearance in the impersonal Youth Court. At the same time it shows the victim that the process is not 'just a slap on the wrist'.

Community service orders also convey a two-way benefit. They aim to teach the offender that reparation can increase skills and change attitudes, while at the same time, the community, and perhaps the victim, directly gain a service. Although only suitable for the less serious areas of offending, it is more cost-effective than jail.

Other attempts to deflect rampant crime include diversional programs such as the Drug Court and the Mental Impairment Court. They seek ways to forge agreements with offenders so that they understand the underlying basic cause of their crimes. These agreements attempt to direct them along a different path. These are not the soft options they may appear, but sensible opportunities to facilitate change and minimise recidivism. Diversionary programs have also been introduced with some success into Aboriginal communities via the Local Justice Initiatives Program. The committees themselves decide what steps need to be taken, depending on local problems.

Both victim and offender desire 'balanced justice', initially perhaps, the former more than the latter. The victim is saying, 'Stop doing this to me, don't do it to anyone else and accept your punishment'. In many cases, what they want most of all is an apology.

Victim awareness training

If the offender can accept responsibility for the offence and apologise sincerely, there might be some hope for change, but normally the situation is not as simple as this. In youth detention centres victims are sometimes afforded the opportunity to talk to groups about their experiences as a victim, which can have surprising results.

In the December 1997 newsletter, Pauline describes being asked by her counsellor whether she would be prepared to tell a group of young offenders at Magill Training Centre what it was like to be a victim.

> I was apprehensive but said yes. Now I am left wondering who is the victim. Me or these young people who looked just like any ordinary young man you would meet on the street or your daughter might be going out with, or for that matter your son. I don't know what I

expected but they actually care about what had happened to me, they apologised for what had happened even though they didn't commit the offence, they even wished me well for the future. Strange, they really cared. By the time the visit was over I wanted to hug all of them, to tell them that it was OK, that their lives really meant something. I just really wanted to bring them all home and give them love. They looked as if they needed it.

Mediation

Mediation between victim and adult offenders can also take place under strict conditions, which include the presence of a counsellor. Both the offender and the victim must be willing to accept the confronting nature of the meeting. It is not for the faint-hearted and it isn't a procedure suitable in all situations. It can take a victim many years to be ready for such a step.

Social factors

We should be targeting the causes of crime as well as challenging criminal behaviour, looking at prevention rather than just reaction. Research indicates that the level of aggression and anti-social behaviour tends to stay at a very similar level from early childhood to the adult years. The areas in which negative influences can occur include biological (family), cultural (parenting), social (role models), economic (poverty and addiction) and educational (school).

Since 10 per cent of offenders commit 50 per cent of the crime, if we get the social science right, we are in with a chance. Although acknowledging that abhorrent behaviour will not be tolerated, if aspects of crime are viewed as a 'disease' which requires diagnosis, treatment and follow-up, then the opportunity exists to make a more lasting impact.

A common view generally accepted by criminologists is that repeated incarceration with little or minimum rehabilitation just increases the recidivism rate. If the media promote this point of view and argue it enthusiastically, the resultant call from the community is for more prisons and longer sentences.

The thug who waves his hands at the media outside the court where he is charged with assault with an offensive weapon while drug-affected and shouts, in answer to a question, 'I don't fink about me victims. I just do what I gotta', doesn't give one cause for optimism – nor help his defence.

Victim support groups continue to be dedicated and concerned and, as has been described by a victim of crime, the aim is to help develop 'victims with attitude, that is, survivors'. Victim Support Service staff and volunteers frequently present research papers at conferences and public talks, conveying information through balanced arguments on crime and its prevention, always presented outside a political or media-driven format. This is not to deny that a core group of criminals exists for whom very little can be done except to lock them up.

Prisoner Assessment Committee

As referred to briefly in an earlier chapter, the Chief Executive Officer continues to represent victims of crime on the PAC, which meets weekly. Appointment to this committee is made by the relevant minister and the committee's role is to prevent further crime by offenders. The committee undertakes the following activities:

- Advocates for integrated victim awareness programs and training

- Influences policy relating to the victim's point of view in pre-release programs

- Argues for non-release of offenders who show no remorse

- Advocates for improved rehabilitation programs

- Approves or rejects home detention applications

- Assesses re-offending risk, security classifications and recommends prison placements.

In 1998 a government-initiated Review of Victims of Crime was undertaken to which VSS contributed on four fronts – in the areas of victim impact statements, declaration of victims' rights, criminal injuries compensation and 'unmet needs', all issues which were taken up in the new *Victims of Crime Act 2001*. An important component of the VSS input was the following statement which refutes a common defence, especially in motor vehicle crashes.

We do not believe that the responsibility for deliberate criminal behaviour should be excused because a person was unaware of what they were doing – especially in such instances as being under the influence of drugs and alcohol. We believe that such a defence is subject to misuse and a way of avoiding the legal consequences and moral responsibilities of criminal behaviour.

The review led to one of the most important pieces of recent legislation, the *Victims of Crime Act 2001* implemented on 1 January 2003, the delay in its implementation caused by a change of government and the time required to draw up the regulations needed to spell out the detail. The new act enshrines victims' rights to information about the prosecution and its outcome, and clarifies how victims should be treated by the police, the courts and other agencies.

The new act emphasises the early settlement of claims but limits compensation to violent offences and those where violence has been threatened, with provision for both physical and psychological injury. The maximum funeral payment has risen from $3000 to $5000 and the government has the power to make other discretionary payments where appropriate. Victims can apply directly to the Attorney-General by writing to the Crown Solicitor's office. (The *Criminal Injuries Compensation Act 1978* still applies to injuries acquired before 2003.)

VSS won the 'rights' battle but the battle for improved compensation was less successful, as illustrated by the more restrictive eligibility definition. South Australia's earlier legislation had been the most inclusive in Australia and recognised that non-violent victimisation could be very traumatic and have a major life impact.

Other areas of legal clarification and benefits focused on compensation for innocent victims of criminal activity rather than on trivial claims have also been the subject of VSS lobbying to government. For example, an increase in fees for lawyers who represent victims of crime, which have not changed since 1988.

This, the year of the twenty-fifth anniversary is a good time to take stock, look back, learn and celebrate. After our celebrations are over we can look forward with anticipation and energy. There is no room for complacency but we can be grateful for what has been achieved to date – thanks to the combined efforts of literally hundreds of people working together.

The Victim Support Service is still the independent, non-government incorporated body it was in the beginning, although the budget is larger and 85 per cent of its funding is derived from the government, some of which is collected through the Victims of Crime Levy. The balance is still raised from subscriptions, donations and bequests, so there is always a certain tension to ensure that expenses will be met.

In spite of the increased support for a greatly expanded range of services, VSS still needs its volunteers to maintain the momentum. It says a great deal for the ongoing leadership of VSS that the organisation is widely perceived as one of great integrity, which advocates tirelessly for victims of crime. That the organisation is consulted when laws on victimology are being redrafted is indicative of the high esteem in which the organisation is held in all sectors of the community, including the police and the judiciary. Moreover, it is a natural source of information to the justice system and provides a necessary service to the community.

John Halsey (previously a Chairman of the Council) has said that one of the great strengths of VSS has been its ability to maintain a bipartisan and balanced approach with all sides of politics.

*   *   *   *

Ray Whitrod died aged 88 on Friday, 12 July 2003 during the writing of this book. John Halsey's 2002 description of his friend makes a fitting tribute:

> Ray is an extremely intelligent person, very politically astute, a very strong person, emphatic but hugely compassionate and innovative as well. You don't often get opportunities in life to be associated with something which is unequivocally good.
>
> VSS is a wonderful case of a very good person having a very good idea and attracting other very good people around it. And growing something that has made a very valuable contribution to the lives of countless, probably hundreds if not thousands of people. Certainly to the criminal justice infrastructure of this state and this nation.

And so say all of us.

In just 25 years VSS has grown from a small, passionate group lobbying for recognition of the existence of crime victims and their human rights, to a sophisticated statewide service delivery organisation. Still demonstrating the passion and commitment of its early members, VSS has become an integrated and indispensable part of the criminal justice system in South

Australia – an enviable achievement and not accomplished by standing in the shadows but by shining a bright light on the needs and rights of crime victims.

After talking to a group of people in 1983 Ray Whitrod was thanked 'for entertaining us'. His response was, in that case, he hadn't really made his point. The aim was not to entertain but to demonstrate a need for action. 'And to achieve discomfort in the listeners so that they are stimulated to do something!' He called it 'reaching out'.

A similar philosophy went into this book. Has it touched you in any way? Have you been a victim of crime or do you know someone who has? Do you need to tell your family how much you care for them or do you need someone to reach out to you? If you do, you know where we are – call us.

Acknowledgments

All books are the result of teamwork to a greater or lesser extent, and this overview of the first twenty-five years of Victim Support Service (VSS) would not have been written without the group of committed people who generously volunteered time, effort and enthusiasm. It really was a team effort and for me, a great privilege.

The Chief Executive Officer of Victim Support Service, Michael Dawson, decided to approach me to write a history after VSS had published one of my short stories in their newsletter and for this I will always be grateful. Fiona Hemstock, the Librarian at VSS, was given the task of contacting me and her gentle and persuasive arguments were impossible to resist! Fiona became the coordinator, computer whiz and the focus of endless requests. (She also cooks a mean low-fat chocolate cake.)

Kevin Fielke, dedicated Court Companion and member of the Board of Management somehow fitted an extensive series of interviews of early and current members and victims of crime into his busy schedule. Extracts from a number of these have been used, and in total, they constitute a valuable oral history of the organisation. Kevin also has potential as a detective – he was able to track difficult-to-contact interviewees and some of the authors of the poems.

Rosemary Huxter was a founding member of VSS and worked as Administrative Officer from 1987 to 1999. She graciously accepted being 'volunteered' because of her phenomenal memory for the faces and names portrayed in VSS photographs and for her ability to spot written historical errors. Rosemary also contributed humour and great affection for VSS and its history.

Joy Carlisle volunteered to transcribe my notes and dictation before realising that my scrawl resembles a spider on a bender. She is exceptionally patient, hardworking, and another computer expert who willingly reset and typed all drafts.

Kelly McLean volunteered as research assistant after a request in the newsletter for someone with library training. A new graduate, she was keen, lively and efficient. When Kelly left to take up a job, Judy Fander filled her place, providing enthusiasm, extensive experience and the ability to find absolutely anything. Kathleen Bambridge was the first volunteer to start collecting and collating material and we thank her.

Michael Dawson and the Manager of Professional Services, David Kerr, provided constant backup whenever it was needed, answering questions and dispensing practical support and encouragement, which was greatly appreciated. What's more, Michael kept smiling even when the anticipated 25-page pamphlet grew into a book.

Thank you to Michael O'Connell, South Australia's first Victims of Crime Coordinator, who went to a great deal of trouble to provide me with legislative information relevant to victims of crime.

Reception/administration staff Tanya Seagrim and Kristina Juraja cheerfully contributed in practical ways, especially when it came to collating, scanning and printing documents.

Victim Support Service wishes to thank Simon Kneebone for permission to print his cartoon on page 88.

On behalf of VSS I would like to acknowledge and thank the following people who agreed to be interviewed for this book and allowed extracts to be printed:

Rebecca Abbott, David Kerr, Judith Barnes, Jan McClelland, Ross Bowles, Myk Mykyta, Jean Chinca, Michael O'Connell, Max Dawson, John Oliphant, Michael Dawson, Andrew Paterson, Trevor Griffin, Ron Penglase, John Halsey, Elke Pfau, Barrie Hibbert, Judi Rea, Des House, Birgitte Sorenson, Rick Hudson, Jan Stevenson, Rosemary Huxter, Christopher Sumner, Harold Weir.

It is difficult to write a non-fiction book without a point of view. Any opinions expressed are mine and not necessarily those of the Victim Support Service.

Facts, extracts and quotations have been checked as thoroughly as possible. With such a highly qualified and enthusiastic resource team it seems fair to take responsibility for any errors, for which I apologise in advance.

A sincere thank-you to all who contributed.

Jo Robinson

Bibliography

Attorney General's Department. (2001). *Victims of Crime Act 2001, South Australia.* Adelaide: Parliament of South Australia.

Colwell, Max & Naylor, Alan. (1981). *Adelaide, an illustrated history.* Joslin, South Australia: McP.

Cornwall, Charles. (2003). *The punishment fit the crime: Memoirs of a probation and parole officer.* Adelaide: Peacock Publications.

Ethnic Radio 5EBI. (1994). *Victim Awareness Week Andrew Paterson talks about Victims of Crime Service.* Adelaide: Ethnic Radio 5EBI.

Funder, Anna. (2002). *Stasiland.* Melbourne: Text Publishing Company Pty Ltd.

Gardner, Julie. (1990). *Victims and criminal justice.* Adelaide: Office of Crime Statistics, South Australian Attorney-General's Department.

Grabosky, Peter. (1981). *Report of the Committee of Inquiry on Victims of Crime, 1981.* Adelaide: Committee of Inquiry on Victims of Crime.

Legal Services Commission. (1999). *The law handbook.* Adelaide, South Australia: Legal Services Commission of South Australia.

Mullen, Paul E., Pathe, Michele & Purcell, Rosemary. (2000). *Stalkers and their victims.* Cambridge, England: Cambridge University Press.

Mykyta, Anne-Marie. (1981). *It's a long way to Truro.* Adelaide: McPhee Gribble.

O'Brien, Bob. (2002). *Young Blood: The story of the family murders.* Sydney: Harper Collins Publishers.

Page, Michael F. (1985). *Colonial South Australia.* South Melbourne: J.M. Dent.

Paterson, Andrew. (1989). *Victim support infrastructures for elderly persons.* Adelaide: Victims of Crime Service.

Paterson, Andrew. (1990). *Services for victims of crime and crime prevention programmes in Europe and the United Kingdom.* United Kingdom: Victims of Crime Service.

Peter Alexander and Associates Pty Ltd. (1996). *Review Victims of Crime Service Inc.* Adelaide.

Salter, Anna C. (2003). *Predators, pedophiles, rapists and other sex offenders.* New York: Basic Books.

South Australian Police Department. (1985). *Victims past, victims future: A South Australian Police Perspective. Adelaide*: SA Police Dept.

Statman, Jan B. (1995). *The battered woman's survival guide: Breaking the cycle.* Maryland: Taylor Trade Publishing.

Victim Support Service Incorporated. (2000). *Victims of crime: Working together to improve services.* Adelaide: South Australian Institute of Justice Studies & Justice Studies Department & Australasian Society of Victimology & Victim Support Service Inc.

Victim Support Service. (1979–2003). Annual reports, council minutes and news-letters. Adelaide: Victim Support Service.

Whitrod, Ray. (2001). *Before I sleep: Memoirs of a modern police officer.* St. Lucia, Queensland: University of Queensland Press.

Zehr, Howard. (2001). *Transcending: Reflections of crime victims – portraits & interviews by Howard Zehr.* Intercourse, US: Good Books.

Victim Support Service Inc

Addresses

11 Halifax Street, Adelaide SA 5000
Telephone (08) 8231 5626
Country Toll Free 1800 182 368
Fax (08) 8231 5458
Email: info@victimsa.org, or
visit our website
www.victimsa.org

15 Riverview Drive, Berri SA 5343
Telephone (08) 8582 2968

5 Mark Street, Mount Gambier SA 5290
Telephone (08) 8723 2968

44 Tassie Street, Port Augusta SA 5700
Telephone (08) 8641 1115

Masonic Lodge, Bligh Street, Port Lincoln SA 5605
Telephone (08) 8683 0111

131B Florence Street, Port Pirie SA 5540
Telephone (08) 8633 4888

Services Available

- Professional counselling, advocacy and support
- Information about victims' rights and criminal injuries compensation claims
- Support groups for crime victims
- Court preparation for adults and children
- Court Companion service
- Training Seminars for professionals who have contact with victims of crime
- Presentations to community groups
- Armed hold-up awareness seminars
- Advocacy for reform to the criminal justice system
- Resource Centre/Library

Brochures

Support Services for Victims of Crime
Court Companion Services
How can you assist a victim of crime
The Impact of House Breaks-ins
Victims of Crime Compensation pre-2003 – Blue
Victims of Crime Compensation post-2002 – Yellow
Volunteering Opportunities
Resource Centre
After Child Trauma group (Adelaide group)
Moving Forwards Women's Group (Adelaide group)
Life After Threat Terror and Endangerment group (Adelaide group)
Your rights as a client
Victim Support Service Language Brochure in the following languages:

- Chinese
- Greek
- Italian
- Serbian
- Vietnamese

Fact Sheets

Home Invasions
Being A Witness In Court
Compensation
After Assault
Coping With Sleeplessness
Common Reactions After A Crime
Trauma and Your Body
Armed Hold Up At Work
Robbery With Violence
Coping Strategies
Managing Anger for Survivors of Crime
I can't believe this is happening
Why Can't I forget? Information for women who were sexually abused
in childhood
Why can't I forget? Information for men who were sexually abused
in childhood
Why can't she forget? Information for partners of women who were sexually
abused in childhood
Information for Employers

Index

151